PERSPECTIVES ON EARLY CHILDHOOD PSYCHOLOGY AND EDUCATION

Volume 9, Issue 1
Spring 2025

Copyright © 2025
Pace University Press
41 Park Row
15th floor
New York, NY 10038

ISBN: 978-1-935625-87-2
ISSN: 2471-1527

Member

Council of Editors of Learned Journals

PERSPECTIVES on EARLY CHILDHOOD PSYCHOLOGY and EDUCATION

EDITOR
Maria Hernández Finch, *Ball State University*

ASSOCIATE EDITORS
Tammy Hughes, *Duquesne University*
Barbara A. Mowder, *Pace University*
Flo Rubinson, *Brooklyn College*
Beth Trammell, *Indiana University East*

EDITORIAL ASSISTANTS
Emma Bauman
Diana Salto

EDITORIAL REVIEW BOARD
Vincent C. Alfonso, *Gonzaga University*
Stefano Bagnato, *University of Pittsburgh*
Renee Bergeron, *Consultant*
Zeynep Biringen, *Colorado State University*
Bruce A. Bracken, *College of William & Mary*
Melissa Bray, *University of Connecticut*
Victoria Comerchero, *Touro College*
Gerard Costa, *Montclair State University*
Grace Elizade-Utnick, *City University of New York at Brooklyn College*
Kathryn Fletcher, *Ball State University*
Gilbert Foley, *New York Center for Child Development*
Laurie Ford, *University of British Columbia*
Pamela Guess, *University of Tennessee*
Robin Hojnoski, *Lehigh University*
Anthony Mangino, *University of Kentucky*
Sara McCane-Bowling, *University of Tennessee*
David McIntosh, *Loyola University Chicago*
Geraldine Oades-Sese, *Rutgers Robert Wood Johnson Medical School*
Matt Reynolds, *University of Kansas*
Gail Ross, *NY Presbyterian Hospital*
Susan Ruby, *Eastern Washington University*
Mark Sossin, *Pace University*
Esther Stavrou, *Yeshiva University*

Mark Terjesen, *St. John's University*
Lea A. Theodore, *College of William and Mary*
Mary Ward, *Weill Cornell Medical College*
Adriana Wissel, *Gonzaga University*

TABLE OF CONTENTS

Editor's Note vii
Maria Hernández Finch

GENERAL ARTICLES:

Practical Applications of Play Therapy Principles in Early Childhood Classrooms... 1
Colleen D. Martinez and Beth A. Trammell

Phenomenological Variant of Ecological Systems Theory (PVEST): Implications for Early Childhood Education 23
Kathryn L. Fletcher and Qunishia N. Carter

An Equity-Based and Culturally Responsive Bill of Rights for Early Childhood Students of Color with Exceptionalities....... 51
Evette Simmons-Reed, Michelle Frazier Trotman Scott, Gloria Taradash, Mildred Boveda, and Donna Y. Ford

Book Review: Addressing Anxiety in Young Learners: A Teacher's Guide to Recognizing Needs and Resolving Behaviors 71
Jacqueline Sperling

LIST OF CONTRIBUTORS 85

EDITORIAL POLICY 91

CALL FOR PAPERS 93

Editor's Note

Maria Hernández Finch

In this issue we feature three articles and a book review that are clarion calls for the field of early childhood psychology and education. As a whole, the articles can be used as topical tutorials. Individually, the articles call for specific expansions in conceptualizations of theory and practice in early childhood.

We would welcome future qualitative, quantitative, systematic review, and Scholarship of Teaching and Learning (SoTL) submissions that expand the literature in each area covered in this issue. Martinez and Trammell (2025) explore play in the classroom setting through a play therapy lens and offer practical case examples for both child and early childhood educator-led play. Fletcher and Carter (2025) advance an invaluable guide to using Spencer's Phenomenological Variant of Ecological Systems Theory (PVEST) in an early childhood context. This important theory is an expansion of Bronfenbrenner's work, and focuses on the unique ways that children, particularly those from minoritized backgrounds, individually experience and interpret contexts differently. Previous work with this theory has focused on older children. The authors succeed in introducing the theory to the early childhood field and in explaining how the theory can be used to expand our understandings of early development in a culturally sustaining manner. Simmons-Reed and colleagues (2025) provide a seminal equity-based and culturally responsive Bill of Rights for children of color with exceptionalities. One of the co-authors, Donna Ford, previously developed a culturally responsive Bill for gifted children of color (Ford et al., 2017).

Major sections of the present article include information on how the pandemic affected rights, advocacy and accountability, access to programming and services, program evaluation and accountability, education, evaluation, and accountability, educators, curriculum and instruction, social and emotional, discipline, families and communities, and access to the internet and technology.

Finally, Sperling (2025) offers a review of a text focused on teachers addressing anxiety in young children in their classrooms. Sperling offers critical analysis based on her expertise as a practitioner and the anxiety literature.

GENERAL ARTICLES

Practical Applications of Play Therapy Principles in Early Childhood Classrooms

Colleen D. Martinez and Beth A. Trammell

Abstract

Play in early childhood is a central tenet to everyday life for children and is thus of great importance to early childhood practitioners. However, the wide variety of definitions, policies, and practices related to play make implementing it effectively in the classroom nuanced. This article explores components of both child-led and adult-led practices—viewed through the lens of play therapy—to aid early childhood educators in applying these practices in the classroom. Case examples from the authors are included to further explore these topics in real-life situations.

Keywords: *play, play therapy, play therapy principles, early childhood, play in classrooms, playful learning*

Practical Applications of Play Therapy Principles in Early Childhood Classrooms

The importance of play in young children's lives has been well-established in the academic literature for decades, but it has also recently gained recognition in the media (Fox, 2007; Hamilton, 2014; Kamenetz, 2018, 2022; Mader, 2022). Play, especially in early childhood, is crucial for nearly every aspect of a child's growth and development. It is how young children communicate, explore, and learn about the world around them. According to the American Academy of Pediatrics, play is about taking risks and testing boundaries, but it also supports brain functioning and strengthens neural connections (Ginsburg & Committee on Psychosocial Aspects of Child and Family Health, 2007; Milteer et al., 2012; Yogman et al., 2018). Play is critical for the development of self-regulation skills and various social competencies, as well as problem-solving and creativity (Johnson et al., 2019). Young children explore their immediate surroundings to learn healthy risk-taking as well as how to build relationships with caregivers. Since play is a critical part of a child's development, it is an important activity that educators can teach, advocate for, and enhance.

Most teachers and practitioners in early childhood spaces recognize the importance of play for young children. However, deciding how to implement play practices in the classroom may be a more convoluted topic, and multiple challenges exist in both the policy and practice of play in early childhood spaces (Parker et al., 2022). Some researchers promote free play, or child-directed play, as an approach that maximizes children's development of pre-kindergarten skills (Aras, 2016; Colliver et al., 2022; Jarvis et al., 2014; Lockhart, 2010), while others find adult-directed, or guided play, to be a more appropriate approach to maximize learning (Toub et al., 2016; Weisberg et al., 2013, Yu et al., 2018). Still others suggest taking an approach that includes open-ended play, modeled play, and purposefully framed play (Edwards et al., 2017). Indeed, a recent review of teachers' views on play-based learning in the early childhood classroom found that although teachers realize the connection between play and learning (Bubikova-Moan et al., 2019), some find it difficult to clearly differentiate free play and learning from learning associated with intentional teacher directives (Pyle & Danniels, 2016). In short, there are a number of ways to engage young children in play to benefit their learning, and teachers perceive play as important, but the approaches that teachers should take to engage young children in play to benefit their learning is less clear.

Historically, early childhood educators have been charged with the task of preparing young children for kindergarten. Researchers and advocates for play have argued that academic readiness and play are not mutually exclusive (Nicolopoulou, 2010; Weisberg et al., 2013; Zosh et al., 2022), and that play is best-suited to prepare young children for academic success (Nicolopoulou, 2010). However, many early childhood educators find it difficult to explain their decision to allow for free play or implement play practices in the classroom. As such, many educators may feel conflicted about how to best prepare their students for the academic rigor of kindergarten while also maintaining a playful learning environment in preschool (Bubikova-Moan, et al., 2019; Fesseha & Pyle, 2016; Sherwood & Reifel, 2013). The continued disagreement regarding the appropriateness of such standards remains an area of contention in the field of early childhood (Allee-Herndon et al., 2019; Almon, 2003; Lynch, 2015).

Because teachers may feel unsure how to implement play, this paper presents two approaches, based on play therapy research, to expose educators to a range of useful methods available for use in their classroom. This paper introduces play therapy, followed by a description of two types of play therapy. These two approaches have been identified by play therapy experts as appropriate for modified use by teachers in the classroom, to expand the application of these techniques in early childhood spaces (Ray, 2023; Tucker et al., 2017). Child- centered play therapy (CCPT) and Theraplay®,[1] are two approaches rooted in the development and maintenance of the relationship between teacher and child, but the manner in which that happens is quite different when implemented in child-led or adult-led play. We then share how these approaches can be applied to the early childhood classroom at an individual-level, as well as within the larger classroom setting. We believe that by sharing two different approaches, teachers can identify which approach makes the most sense for their classroom. We are not advocating for early childhood educators to provide mental health services. Rather, we are suggesting that some principles and methods of play therapy can be additional resources and tools for early childhood educators, to have as a framework for increasing their play proficiency and deepening the teacher-child relationship.

Brief Introduction to Play Therapy

Working from the premise that play is the language of the child (Landreth, 2023), play therapy practitioners use play and

---

[1] Theraplay is a registered service mark of The Theraplay® Institute, Chicago, IL, USA.

expressive, creative, and playful activities to address the social, emotional, and developmental needs of children. The Association for Play Therapy was founded in 1982 to build connections among mental health professionals who were using play in their work with children (Association for Play Therapy [APT], 2024a). The APT defines play therapy as "the systematic use of a theoretical model to establish an interpersonal process wherein trained play therapists use the therapeutic powers of play to help clients prevent or resolve psychosocial difficulties and achieve optimal growth and development" (APT, 1997, p.7). Play therapy is not simply the act of playing with a child, or allowing a child to play; rather, play therapy occurs in the context of a safe and supportive relationship wherein the practitioner values the child and their natural language: play. Play therapy is used skillfully and strategically, within a theoretical framework, to achieve specific goals. In order to earn a play therapist credential, applicants must be licensed mental health professionals, school counselors, or school psychologists, and they must complete within a timeframe of two to ten years a rigorous process which includes a specified number of hours of play therapy training, play therapy supervision, and supervised play therapy experience (APT, 2024b).

Although early childhood educators are unlikely to be play therapists and will not be delivering therapy per se, these play therapy principles, practices, and skills have been identified as potentially useful to educators in their work with young students (Ray, 2023; Tucker et al., 2017). While there are many ways to use play in therapy, the APT recognizes the most well- researched and time-tested seminal theories and historically significant approaches, among them being child-centered play therapy (CCPT) and Theraplay (APT, 2024c). Next, we will explore each of these approaches and use case examples from our clinical practices to highlight their usefulness in early childhood spaces.

Child-Centered Play Therapy

CCPT is one of the oldest and most empirically tested forms of play therapy. Within the context of a fully accepting therapeutic relationship, the child is given the opportunity to safely process their experiences and feelings. Virginia Axline, who developed CCPT, began her work as a classroom teacher in the 1940s and later became a student of Carl Rogers. As a teacher, she saw that children benefited from having a trusting relationship with an adult in the classroom, and she observed that they communicated through play. Like Rogers, she believed that people are innately driven toward achieving psychological wellness. As a second-grade classroom teacher, she published a paper about using play-based therapeutic interventions with students impacted by war (Axline, 1944). She eventually became a clinical psychologist and adapted Rogers' non-directive principles of psychotherapy in her work with children to develop non-directive play therapy, which is now referred to as CCPT (Landreth, 1993).

Axline (1947) outlined eight basic principles that guide the therapist in centering the child:

1. The therapist must develop a warm, friendly relationship with the child, in which good rapport is established as soon as possible.
2. The therapist accepts the child exactly as he is.
3. The therapist establishes a feeling of permissiveness in the relationship so that the child feels free to express his feelings completely.
4. The therapist is alert to recognize the feelings the child is expressing and reflects those feelings back to him in such a manner that he gains insight into his behavior.
5. The therapist maintains a deep respect for the child's ability to solve his own problems if given an opportunity to do so. The responsibility to make choices and institute change is the child's.

6. The therapist does not attempt to direct the child's actions or conversation in any manner. The child leads the way; the therapist follows.
7. The therapist does not attempt to hurry the therapy along. It is a gradual process and is recognized as such by the therapist.
8. The therapist establishes only those limitations that are necessary to anchor the therapy to the world of reality and to make the child aware of his responsibility in the relationship. (pp. 73–74)

Axline's principles emphasize that CCPT is completely child-directed—the therapist does not ask questions, lead the play, or focus on problems. Instead, the therapist provides a safe relationship and a play space in which the child can explore and engage with the toys and play materials. The therapist completely accepts the child and only sets limits when necessary to preserve the safety of the child, the therapist, and the toys. In the context of such a relationship, the child explores, expresses, and develops a sense of value and competence. They grow, process issues, and gain mastery. When the therapist remains child-centered, the therapy can focus on what the child needs—not what the therapist *believes* the child needs. Although the therapist does not lead the session in child-centered play therapy, there are specific techniques that the therapist implements, which include tracking behavior, reflecting content, reflecting feeling, returning responsibility, facilitating creativity, esteem building/encouragement, facilitating relationship, and limit setting (Ray, 2004).

While CCPT originally involved only the child and therapist, practitioners have adapted it to harness the power of relationship with others in the child's life. It has been adapted for use with parents in filial therapy (Guerney, 1964; VanFleet, 2011) and child-parent relationship therapy (CPRT; Bratton et al., 2006), and also for use with teachers in child-teacher relationship training (Morrison & Helker, 2010). CCPT is typically used with children aged three to 10 years old, and it is used in both individual and group settings (Ray,

2011). Numerous studies have indicated the effectiveness of CCPT in decreasing children's emotional and behavioral problems (Blalock et al., 2019; Burgin & Ray, 2022; Ray et al., 2022), and it is rated as a promising practice by the Title IV-E Prevention Services Clearinghouse (2022) and the California Evidence-Based Clearinghouse for Child Welfare (2021).

Theraplay and Sunshine Circles

While CCPT is on the non-directive, or child-directed, end of the spectrum of play therapies, whereby the child is the leader of the interaction, Theraplay is situated on the other end of that spectrum with adults in a directive role. Theraplay is an adult-directed, relationship-focused, and physically active play therapy intervention that has its theoretical foundation in attachment theory and neurodevelopmental theory. Theraplay was developed in the late 1960s by Phyllis Booth and Ann Jernberg (Booth & Jernberg, 2010), who provided psychological services for Chicago's newly developed Head Start program. Among the thousands of preschool children in the program they were responsible for, hundreds presented with emotional and behavioral challenges. While working with these very young children, Booth and Jernberg developed interventions that were play-based. Since the methods they used were very different from those used in earlier types of play therapy, they called the intervention Theraplay. Like CCPT, Theraplay is rated as a promising practice by the California Evidence-Based Clearinghouse for Child Welfare (2023).

In Theraplay sessions, the adult is a playful, sensitive, and responsive leader. The child is cared for and regulated by the adult, overcomes developmentally appropriate challenges in games and activities, and gains a sense of accomplishment. Goals include enhancing attachment, increasing self-regulation, and promoting trust and joyful engagement (Booth & Jernberg, 2010). The four dimensions of Theraplay—Structure, Nurture, Challenge, and Engage—provide a framework for sessions that replicate the kind of nurturing and playful interactions that healthy parents have with their very young children, where the child is seen, valued, and attended to, and lead to healthy attachments. Consciously using tone of voice, eye contact, touch, repetition, and rhythm fosters a safe and joyful connection between parent and child.

Regulation is a priority in Theraplay; clinicians use interactive regulation, up-regulating activities, and down-regulating activities to promote co-regulation and eventually the child's self-regulation. Up-regulating activities are typically more active, physical, fast-paced, and loud. A classic example of up-regulating is a game of singing "Ring Around the Rosie." Singing together while holding hands and moving in a circle, eventually falling down together, can raise the energy level. Down-regulating activities are typically quieter, slower, and less active. For example, the adult playing a call and response "repeat after me" game, where their voice starts out loud and ends in a whisper, might be down regulating. When the adult remains regulated in interaction with the child despite challenges or stressors, and the adult remains connected, responsive, and maintains safety, the child is regulated by the adult. Over time, the child who remains regulated through up- and down-regulating activities develops a greater ability to self-regulate.

Theraplay has been adapted into Group Theraplay and Sunshine Circles (Tucker et al., 2017). Group Theraplay is also provided by a mental health professional, but rather than treating a parent–child dyad, the treatment is offered to a group. Group Theraplay uses the same four dimensions as regular Theraplay, with the aim of developing playful, nurturing, well-regulated connections and a sense of belonging among the members. Studies on the impact of Group Theraplay on children are relatively few, but they have found evidence of improvements in social communication and behavior problems (Sancak, 2019; Siu, 2014).

Sunshine Circles are based on Group Theraplay, but they can be administered by adults who are not necessarily mental health professionals, such as early childhood educators. Sunshine Circles can be used with an entire general education, inclusion, or special education class, as all students can benefit from the active and joyful engagement, and the objectives of these adult-led playgroups are aligned with the state social and emotional learning standards in the common core (Theraplay, 2014). In Sunshine Circles, teachers and other helpers lead students in a series of activities and simple games meant to foster fun, connection, and cooperation in the classroom.

Three rules guide Sunshine Circles and communicate the gathering's priorities: "No Hurts, Stick Together, and Have Fun" (Schieffer, 2019, p. 34). In the process of a Sunshine Circle, the class is broken down into smaller groups, each led by the teacher and other helpers such as teacher's assistants, to provide students with much needed individual attention. By participating in weekly Sunshine Circles throughout the school year, children come to understand that they will be safe and cared for, they will be noticed, appreciated and connected, and they will experience joyful interactions when they follow the adults' lead in the sessions. Studies have found that Sunshine Circles decrease behavior problems and improve social skills, and they also improve teacher-student relationships (Tucker et al., 2017; Tucker et al., 2021). In the following sections, we will explore how to apply some play therapy principles and skills using CCPT and Sunshine Circles in early childhood classrooms, and present case examples to provide educators with more tools to enhance relationships, decrease emotional and behavioral problems, and facilitate learning and development in their classrooms.

Applying Child-Centered Play Therapy Skills in the Classroom

In Dee Ray's (2023) recently published book, *Playful Education: Using Playful Strategies to Elevate Your Classroom*, she proposes that educators can use the PlayBreaks model to apply CCPT concepts in early childhood classrooms. In PlayBreaks, the teacher provides the "child of focus" (Ray, 2023, p. 69), meaning a child of concern who is chosen because they might benefit from an accepting relational experience, with access to a designated play space in the classroom or a separate playroom for 20-minute sessions once per week for six weeks. The play space in the classroom (or separate playroom) is equipped with a variety of thoughtfully selected toys and materials that can allow for expression in the following categories: family/nurturing, scary, expressive, pretend/fantasy, and aggressive (Ray, 2023). Over the course of six weeks, the teacher uses CCPT skills—*tracking behavior, reflecting content, reflecting feeling, returning responsibility, facilitating creativity, esteem-building/encouragement, facilitating relationship,* and *limit setting*—to provide the child with an attentive, accepting, understanding, and empowering experience (Ray, 2023). Through the experience of PlayBreaks, the child and teacher benefit from an improved relationship and the teacher develops a deeper understanding of the child through their play. Ray has proposed that when teachers become more experienced in providing individual PlayBreaks, they are able to implement the child-centered skills with the entire class in the classroom, thereby creating a more playful and emotionally attuned classroom culture. The following is a case example from the first author's experiences of implementing CCPT and providing consultation to a teacher in a preschool classroom.

Classroom Example of PlayBreaks

Four-year-old Zyon (all names in the examples are pseudonyms, and the material has been changed to protect confidentiality), who had recently moved out of a domestic violence shelter with his mother, was a challenging student in Mrs. Murphy's preschool classroom. He often exhibited aggressive and controlling behavior, frequently refused to follow adult directions, and would push and kick his classmates and grab items out of their hands. The teacher's usual behavioral interventions, including redirection, praise, rewards, and consequences, were not effective in decreasing Zyon's misbehavior.

Mrs. Murphy began to meet with Zyon for weekly PlayBreaks in the classroom while the rest of the students went to music class. In

Practical Applications of Play Therapy Principles

these weekly sessions, Mrs. Murphy did not ask questions, did not focus on Zyon's misbehavior, and did not attempt to direct his play in any way. She was attentive, accepting, and demonstrated CCPT skills as Zyon played. Although he had access to a variety of toys and play materials, Zyon usually chose to play with a family of dolls and a jump rope. He would often take the mother and child dolls under a table and pull chairs in around them so that they were hidden. Mrs. Murphy would *track behavior* and make statements such as "You took them and went under the table." When it was difficult for Zyon to pull the chairs under the table exactly how he wanted them to fit, she would use *esteem-building/encouragement* by saying "You're not giving up!" And when he arranged the chairs how he had wanted, she would say "You did it, just the way you wanted to." When Zyon whispered that he and the dolls were hiding, she would *reflect content* by saying "All of you are hiding under there," and when he hid his face and looked worried, she would *reflect feeling* by saying "It's scary hiding out in there."

Throughout the course of the PlayBreaks, Zyon played out a scene in which he, a mother doll, and a boy doll hid from something scary by going under the table. When Zyon wanted Mrs. Murphy to engage in play with him, she wanted to be sure that Zyon was leading the play, so she used the whisper technique (Landreth, 2023) by asking Zyon for direction in a whisper: "What should I do?" Zyon eventually directed Mrs. Murphy in play where he took her under the table to hide, and he used a jump rope as a whip to protect them both from an invisible intruder. Mrs. Murphy said, "You decided to use the rope as a whip to protect us," to *return responsibility* and highlight Zyon's ability to make decisions in order to highlight the relationship between him and her, thereby *facilitating relationship*.

In his last PlayBreak, Zyon pretended to fly around the room like a superhero. He wanted to tie the jump rope around his neck as a cape, but out of concern for his safety, Mrs. Murphy used the ACT model of *limit setting* (Landreth, 2023). Mrs. Murphy (A) acknowledged the feeling by saying "Zyon, you would like to tie the rope around your neck so you can have a cape," then (C) communicated the limit, "the rope isn't for tying around your neck," and (T) targeted an alternative by saying "You can use a long line of paper towels or my scarf as a cape instead." Zyon used a long line of paper towels tucked into the top of his t-shirt and triumphantly "flew" around the room. Using the ACT model of limit setting helped Mrs. Murphy to be more accepting of Zyon while also maintaining his safety, and she helped Zyon to learn more acceptable ways to get his needs met.

In his PlayBreaks with Mrs. Murphy, Zyon appeared to process his very early experiences of domestic violence, and Mrs. Murphy's understanding of Zyon grew tremendously. By seeing Zyon in a different light—not as a difficult boy with behavior problems but as a little boy who felt the need to take control in order to feel safe—her approach to him in the classroom became more empathic. Zyon's sense of connection with Mrs. Murphy remained strong and positive even after his PlayBreaks had ended, resulting in a more cooperative and less challenging classroom experience for the rest of the school year. Mrs. Murphy met with other students in PlayBreaks after Zyon had his sessions, and she continued to use CCPT skills with all of the students in her class. She remarked on how much more effective she was in her relationship with Zyon after their experience of PlayBreaks.

Applying Theraplay and Sunshine Circles Dimensions in the Classroom

The dimensions of Theraplay and the rules of Sunshine Circles can be helpful to educators and clinicians in their work with young children. The "Structure" dimension reminds us that young children benefit from environments that are safe and predictable. Therefore, adults provide direction, create order, and carefully attend to transitions so that children know what to expect and what is expected of them. Adults incorporate rhythm, routine, and repetition. They maintain their own regulation and co-regulate children by using a playful tone of voice, gestures, and gentle grounding touch to provide guidance without using too many words.

Practical Applications of Play Therapy Principles

The "Nurture" dimension acknowledges every child's need for nurturing connection. Adults use tone of voice, eye contact, smiles, and gentle nurturing touch to convey a sense of appreciation and care for each child. Welcoming each child by name and providing individual attention, gentle caring touch, and small snacks make children feel seen, valued, and attended to.

To incorporate the "Challenge" dimension, adults lead individual games and activities with a titrated amount of difficulty and scaffolded support so that children are challenged, are successful, and feel a sense of accomplishment. Children cooperate with each other and develop a sense of teamwork.

The "Engage" dimension reminds adults to be playful and encourages them to interact with children in ways that allow both adults and children to connect, have fun, and share joy. Adults strategically incorporate games and activities that children will want to engage in so that adults and children enjoy their interactions and develop more positive relationships overall. The rules of Sunshine Circles—"No Hurts, Stick Together, and Have Fun" (Schieffer, 2019, p.34)—which can be used in any classroom, session, or gathering with children, reinforce the priorities of nurturance and safety, connection, and joy. The following is the first author's case example of applying Sunshine Circles in a preschool classroom.

Classroom Example of Sunshine Circles

An inclusion preschool classroom of four-year-olds presented several challenges, including aggression and physical acting out from a number of students, a lack of cooperation with classroom routines, and a lack of a sense of cohesion among the students. These challenges led to a feeling of being overwhelmed and frustrated on the part of the classroom assistants and at times on the part of the skilled and experienced teacher, Ms. Solo, as well.

For example, one student named Adam exhibited aggressive behavior on a regular basis, often hitting and kicking when asked to do things he did not want to do. Another student, Conor, was apprehensive, sedentary, and mostly non-verbal at school, although his parents reported that he spoke fluently at home. He would regularly sit silently rather than interact or follow directions. Sandra, who had been diagnosed as being on the autism spectrum, was a student who often appeared happy but rarely spoke at home, never spoke at school, and usually required physical prompting because she did not follow verbal directions or routines. By contrast, Iris was a playful student who was quite verbal—she often spoke for her classmates and took over during tasks and in play when they struggled.

With the varying needs and challenges present in the classroom, the tone of the assistants and the classroom was often more authoritarian and rigid than Ms. Solo wanted, and the classroom lacked the joy and playful engagement which she strived to achieve. Ms. Solo began running a weekly Sunshine Circle in the class. Each week at the same time, she led the students and assistants in a series of songs, playful games, and activities. The initial Sunshine Circle was about 10 minutes long and only included a few games and activities. Over time, as the students became more familiar with the routines and became more deeply engaged, additional songs, games, and activities were introduced, and over the course of the school year, the sessions eventually lasted 30 minutes. A typical Sunshine Circle later in the school year would include the following activities:

- A welcome song, sung by everyone as they gathered (and eventually held hands) in a circle while providing eye contact and smiles to each person.
- "Ring Around the Rosie," ending with everyone sitting down at the same time together in a circle.
- Singing a song where each student is mentioned by name, and everyone claps along in rhythm.
- A reminder of the rules: No Hurts, Stick Together, Have Fun!
- Small group time, where students were divided into groups with one adult each.

Practical Applications of Play Therapy Principles

- Small group check-ins, where adults provided individualized nurturing attention to each child in their small group, including checking for "owies" or "special spots," such as a scratch or a freckle on the hand.
- A small group nurturing activity where the adults in each small group sang a brief song and provided a small snack to each child in the small group individually.
- A whole-group cooperation and challenge game, such as passing around a stuffed animal while singing a song together.
- An individual challenge activity, such as one student popping a bubble while the others waited their turn.
- A whole-group song with gentle physical interaction, such as singing "Row, Row, Row, Your Boat" while holding hands and rocking together.
- A goodbye song.
- A structured transition to the next classroom activity, such as by having all students wearing white shoes go to the next activity first, followed by all students wearing brown shoes, etc.

Ms. Solo and her assistants found that the students enjoyed the nurturing check-ins tremendously. The adults saw how eager the students were for one-on-one attention as they rubbed their hands with lotion or counted their freckles with the gentle touch of a cotton ball. In this low-stakes environment where they did not need to have the children perform academic tasks, the adults felt less pressure and enjoyed these positive interactions with the children.

Adam very much enjoyed Ms. Solo gently counting his freckles with a cotton ball, and he spontaneously noticed that Conor had these "special spots," too. Adam asked if he could count Conor's special spots, and he very gently pressed a cotton ball into the freckles on Conor's hand. Although he was startled at first, Conor's relieved and grateful smile showed that he enjoyed this gentle and nurturing interaction with a classmate who had often intimidated him in the past.

Sandra particularly enjoyed rhythmic and physical play. Singing "Row, Row, Row, Your Boat" was one of her favorite activities, and while she did not sing along, she often smiled and spontaneously responded to eye contact. Her first time speaking at school was after a round of the song where she said in an excited voice, "Sandra happy!" Iris struggled with wanting to take over for Conor when playing the "pass the stuffed animal" game. With gentle encouragement, she stayed in her place in the circle while Conor eventually took the stuffed toy and, ever so slowly, passed it to the next child. The group spontaneously responded in applause when, for the first time, every child in the group participated and the toy made its way around the circle.

Over the course of the year, the songs and routines became familiar to the students, and their enjoyment of the games and activities resulted in more cooperative and positive interactions. The adults in the classroom also gave more one-on-one attention to the students. Students' enjoyment of the nurturing interactions resulted in the adults being more comfortable and confident in providing gentle and playful care to them, which resulted in students who were more responsive to direction. Turn-taking and shared enjoyment were observed more frequently among the students, and levels of aggression decreased. The tone of the classroom felt more positive and playful throughout the week, even outside of the Sunshine Circles.

Overall, the Sunshine Circles led the adults in the room to become more playful and nurturing in their interactions and the students to become more engaged and cooperative. The adults exhibited more confidence in their ability to lead the students in a fun and playful way. Although the assistants had initially expressed some skepticism about having non-academic, play-based sessions during the school day, they later found that the engagement, positivity, and cooperation fostered during the Sunshine Circles resulted in students who were more ready to learn throughout the rest of the week. As a result, the classroom gained the sense of joy and playful engagement to which Ms. Solo had aspired.

Concluding Remarks

It is hoped that this brief introduction to two modalities with roots in play therapy inspires future teachers and clinicians to continue learning about how play and play therapy principles can be leveraged in early childhood settings, to provide more effective and developmentally appropriate care to young children. However, this paper is not meant to be a substitute for training. If teachers are going to use new play-based methods in schools, it will be important for them to receive training, mentoring, and ongoing professional development. Teachers may also consider engaging in reflective practices, such as journaling and joining a professional learning community. We encourage readers who wish to learn more about these modalities to seek out resources to increase their competency and confidence. The University of North Texas Center for Play Therapy (CPT) offers access to CCPT, group CCPT, and CPRT information, resources, and training on their website (https://cpt.unt.edu/), and the Theraplay Institute (TTI) provides access to Theraplay, Group Theraplay, and Sunshine Circles information, resources, and training on their website (https://theraplay.org/). Those who are interested in learning more can view streaming videos, attend live webinars and in-person training, and receive supervision. It would be important to have at least one trained and certified teacher who can provide training, supervision, and mentoring to others using these play-based methods in a school. Those seeking to become certified practitioners can complete rigorous processes which require training, experience, and supervision.

There are also resources available for faculty and students who are not able to pursue training and supervision at this time but who would like to incorporate CCPT, Theraplay, and Sunshine Circles principles into their work. University of North Texas CPT provides photos and a video of CCPT playrooms, a list of toys and materials for a fully equipped playroom, and guidance on how to select playroom materials on their website. They also offer several publications for purchase, including Dee Ray's books, *Advanced Play Therapy* (2011), which contains her CCPT treatment manual, and *Playful Education* (2023), which specifically addresses how to apply CCPT principles in the classroom in the form of PlayBreaks. TTI offers publications on their website, including the *Sunshine Circles Teacher Resource Manual*, books containing Theraplay activities, a song book, and videos. TTI has also posted 20 videos on its YouTube page (https://www.youtube.com/@TheraplayIn), including demonstrations of songs and activities.

It is important to note that teachers will need to gain significant buy-in when implementing any new methods. Teachers will need to justify the investment of time and resources. While the need for new materials may be relatively minimal, student and teacher time during the school day is a precious commodity. Sharing research findings on the impact of these practices on the classroom and on academic achievement may assist teachers in making the appeal to administrators and parents. Similarly, new play-based methods, especially those that involve touch, may require not only administrative permission but also parental consent. Teachers should consult with their administrators, and develop policies and procedures around parental consent on the student level for Play Breaks and on the classroom level for Sunshine Circles.

References

Allee-Herndon, K. A., Dillman Taylor, D., & Roberts, S. K. (2019). Putting play in its place: Presenting a continuum to decrease mental health referrals and increase purposeful play in classrooms. *International Journal of Play, 8*(2), 186–203. https://doi.org/10.1080/21594937.2019.1643993

Almon, J. (2003). The vital role of play in early childhood education. In S. Olfman (Ed.), *All work and no play…How educational reforms are harming our preschoolers* (pp. 17–42). Praeger Publishers/Greenwood Publishing Group.

Aras, S. (2016). Free play in early childhood education: A phenomenological study. *Early Child Development and Care, 186*(7), 1173–1184. https://doi.org/10.1080/03004430.2015.1083558

Association for Play Therapy. (1997). A definition of play therapy. *The Association for Play Therapy Newsletter, 16*(1), 7.

Association for Play Therapy. (2024a, April 24). *About APT.* https://www.a4pt.org/page/AboutAPT

Association for Play Therapy. (2024b, April 24). *Credentials.* https://www.a4pt.org/general/custom.asp?page=CredentialsInfo

Association for Play Therapy. (2024c, April 24). *RPT standards.* https://cdn.ymaws.com/www.a4pt.org/resource/resmgr/credentials/standards_&_applications/rpt_standards.pdf

Axline, V. M. (1944). Morale on the school front. *The Journal of Educational Research, 37*(7), 521–533.

Axline, V. M. (1947). *Play therapy: The Inner Dynamics of Childhood.* Ballantine. Blalock, S. M., Lindo, N., & Ray, D. C. (2019). Individual and group child-centered play therapy: Impact on social-emotional competencies. *Journal of Counseling & Development, 97*(3), 238–249. https://doi.org/10.1002/jcad.12264

Booth, P. B., & Jernberg, A. M. (2010). *Theraplay: Helping parents and children build better relationships through attachment-based play.* John Wiley & Sons.

Bratton, S. C., Landreth, G. L., Kellam, T., & Blackard, S. R. (2006). *Child parent relationship therapy (CPRT) treatment manual: A 10-session filial therapy model for training parents.* Routledge/Taylor & Francis Group.

Bubikova-Moan, J., Næss Hjetland, H., & Wollscheid, S. (2019). ECE teachers' views on play- based learning: A systematic review. *European Early Childhood Education Research Journal, 27*(6), 776–800. https://doi.org/10.1080/1350293X.2019.1678717

Burgin, E. E., & Ray, D. C. (2022). Child-centered play therapy and childhood depression: An effectiveness study in schools. *Journal of Child and Family Studies, 31*, 293–307. https://doi.org/10.1007/s10826-021-02198-6

California Evidence-Based Clearinghouse for Child Welfare. (2021, October). *Child-centered play therapy.* Retrieved June 16, 2024, from https://www.cebc4cw.org/program/child-centered-play-therapy-ccpt/

California Evidence-Based Clearinghouse for Child Welfare. (2023, July). *Level one Theraplay & MIM.* Retrieved June 16, 2024, from https://www.cebc4cw.org/program/theraplay/

Colliver, Y., Harrison, L. J., Brown, J. E., & Humburg, P. (2022). Free play predicts self-regulation years later: Longitudinal evidence from a large Australian sample of toddlers and preschoolers. *Early Childhood Research Quarterly, 59*, 148–161. https://doi.org/10.1016/j.ecresq.2021.11.011

Edwards, S., Cutter-Mackenzie, A., Moore, D., & Boyd, W. (2017). Finding the balance: A play framework for play-based learning and intentional teaching in early childhood education. *Every Child, 23*(1), 14–15. Early Childhood Australia. https://thespoke.earlychildhoodaustralia.org.au/finding-the-balance/

Fesseha, E., & Pyle, A. (2016). Conceptualising play-based learning from kindergarten teachers' perspectives. *International Journal of Early Years Education, 24*(3), 361-377. https://doi.org/10.1080/09669760.2016.1174105

Fox, J. E. (2007). Back-to-basics: Play in early childhood. *Early Childhood News*, 12–15.

Ginsburg, K. R., & Committee on Psychosocial Aspects of Child and Family Health. (2007). The importance of play in promoting healthy child development and maintaining strong parent-child bonds. *Pediatrics, 119*(1), 182–191. https://doi.org/10.1542/peds.2006-2697

Guerney, B. G., Jr. (1964). Filial therapy: Description and rationale. *Journal of Consulting Psychology, 28*(4), 303–310.

Hamilton, J. (2014, August 6). *Scientists say child's play helps build a better brain*. NPR. https://www.npr.org/sections/ed/2014/08/06/336361277/scientists-say-childs-play-helps-build-a-better-brain

Jarvis, P., Newman, S., & Swiniarski, L. (2014). On "becoming social": The importance of collaborative free play in childhood. *International Journal of Play, 3*(1), 53–68. https://doi.org/10.1080/21594937.2013.863440

Johnson, J. E., Sevimli-Celik, S., Al-Mansour, M. A., Tunçdemir, T. B. A., & Dong, P. I. (2019). Play in early childhood education. In *Handbook of research on the education of young children* (pp. 165–175). Taylor and Francis. https://doi.org/10.4324/9780429442827-12

Kamenetz, A. (2018, August 31). *5 proven benefits of play*. NPR. https://www.npr.org/sections/ed/2018/08/31/642567651/5-proven-benefits-of-play

Kamenetz, A. (2022, February 10). *A top researcher says it's time to rethink our entire approach to preschool*. NPR. https://www.npr.org/2022/02/10/1079406041/researcher-says-rethink-prek-preschool-prekindergarten

Landreth, G. L. (1993). Child-centered play therapy. *Elementary School Guidance & Counseling, 28*(1), 17–29.

Landreth, G. L. (2023). *Play therapy: The art of the relationship* (4th ed.). Routledge.

Lockhart, S. (2010). Play: An important tool for cognitive development. *HighScope Extensions, 24*(3), 1–17.

Lynch, M. (2015). More play please: The perspectives of kindergarten teachers on play in the classroom. *American Journal of Play, 7*(3), 347–370. https://files.eric.ed.gov/fulltext/EJ1070249.pdf

Mader, J. (2022, November 14). *Want resilient and well-adjusted kids? Let them play*. Hechinger Report. https://hechingerreport.org/want-resilient-and-well-adjusted-kids-let-them-play/

Milteer, R. M., Ginsburg, K. R., Council on Communications and Media Committee on Psychosocial Aspects of Child and Family Health (2012). The importance of play in promoting healthy child development and maintaining strong parent-child bond: Focus on children in poverty. *Pediatrics, 129*(1), e204–e213. https://doi.org/10.1542/peds.2011-2953

Morrison, M. O., & Helker, W. P. (2010). Child-teacher relationship training: Using the power of the child-teacher relationship as a school-based mental health intervention. In A. A. Drewes & C. E. Schaefer (Eds.), *School-based play therapy* (2nd ed., pp. 181–195). John Wiley & Sons, Inc.

Nicolopoulou, A. (2010). The alarming disappearance of play from early childhood education. *Human Development, 53*(1), 1–4. https://www.jstor.org/stable/26764938

Parker, R., Thomsen, B. S., & Berry, A. (2022). Learning through play at school–A framework for policy and practice. *Frontiers in Education, 7*. https://doi.org/10.3389/feduc.2022.751801

Pyle, A., & Danniels, E. (2016). A continuum of play-based learning: The role of the teacher in play-based pedagogy and the fear of hijacking play. *Early Education and Development, 28*(3), 274–289. https://doi.org/10.1080/10409289.2016.1220771

Ray, D. (2004). Supervision of basic and advanced skills in play therapy. *Journal of Professional Counseling: Practice, Theory & Research, 32*(2), 28–41.

Ray, D. (2011). *Advanced play therapy: Essential conditions, knowledge, and skills for child practice*. Routledge.

Ray, D. C. (2023). *Playful education: Using play therapy strategies to elevate your classroom*. Routledge.

Ray, D. C., Burgin, E., Gutierrez, D., Ceballos, P., & Lindo, N. (2022). Child-centered play therapy and adverse childhood experiences: A randomized controlled trial. *Journal of Counseling & Development, 100*(2), 134–145. https://doi.org/10.1002/jcad.12412

Sancak, S. (2019). *Effects of group Theraplay on social skills and problem behaviors of preschoolers in classroom environment* [Unpublished master's thesis]. Middle East Technical University.

Schieffer, K. (2019). *Sunshine Circles®: Interactive playgroups for social skills development and classroom management. Teacher resource manual* (2nd ed.). The Theraplay Institute.

Sherwood, S. A., & Reifel, S. (2013). Valuable and unessential: the paradox of preservice teachers' beliefs about the role of play in learning. *Journal of Research in Childhood Education, 27*(3), 267-282. https://doi.org/10.1080/02568543.2013.795507

Siu, A. F. (2014). Effectiveness of group Theraplay® on enhancing social skills among children with developmental disabilities. *International Journal of Play Therapy, 23*(4), 187-203. https://doi.org/10.1037/a0038158

Theraplay. (2014, May 30). Sunshine Circles. [Video]. YouTube. https://www.youtube.com/watch?v=NupTMfVqQA4

Title IV-E Prevention Services Clearinghouse. (2022, December). *Child-centered play therapy*. Retrieved June 16, 2024, from https://preventionservices.acf.hhs.gov/programs/626/show

Toub, T. S., Rajan, V., Golinkoff, R. M., & Hirsh-Pasek, K. (2016). Guided play: A solution to the play versus learning dichotomy. In: D. Geary& D. Berch (Eds.), *Evolutionary perspectives on child development and education* (pp. 117–141). Springer.

Tucker, C., Schieffer, K., Lenz, S., & Smith, S. (2021). Sunshine Circles: Randomized controlled trial of an attachment-based play group with preschool students who are at-risk. *Journal of Child and Adolescent Counseling, 7*(3), 161–175. https://doi.org/10.1080/23727810.2021.1940658

Tucker, C., Schieffer, K., Wills, T. J., Hull, C., & Murphy, Q. (2017). Enhancing social-emotional skills in at-risk preschool students through Theraplay based groups: The Sunshine Circle model. *International Journal of Play Therapy, 26*(4), 185-195. https://doi.org/10.1037/pla0000054

VanFleet, R. (2011). Filial therapy: Strengthening family relationships with the power of play. In C. E. Schaefer (Ed.), *Foundations of play therapy* (2nd ed., pp. 153–169). Wiley.

Weisberg, D. S., Hirsh-Pasek, K., & Golinkoff, R. M. (2013). Guided play: Where curricular goals meet a playful pedagogy. *Mind, Brain, and Education, 7*(2), 104-112. https://doi.org/10.1111/mbe.12015

Yogman, M., Garner, A., Hutchinson, J., Hirsh-Pasek, K., Golinkoff, R. M., Committee on Psychosocial Aspects of Child and Family Health & Council on Communications and Media (2018). The power of play: A pediatric role in enhancing development in young children. *Pediatrics, 142*(3). :e20182058. https://doi.org/10.1542/peds.2018-2058

Yu, Y., Shafto, P., Bonawitz, E., Yang, S. C. H., Golinkoff, R. M., Corriveau, K. H., Hirsh-Pasek, K, Xu, F. (2018). The theoretical and methodological opportunities afforded by guided play with young children. *Frontiers in Psychology, 9*, article 1152. doi: 10.3389/fpsyg.2018.01152

Zosh, J. M., Gaudreau, C., Golinkoff, R. M., & Hirsh-Pasek, K. (2022). The power of playful learning in the early childhood setting. *Young Children, 77*(2), 6-13. https://www.naeyc.org/resources/pubs/yc/summer2022/power-playful-learning

Phenomenological Variant of Ecological Systems Theory (PVEST): Implications for Early Childhood Education

Kathryn L. Fletcher and Qunishia N. Carter

In contemporary industrialized societies, there is no doubt that belonging to a marginalized group (i.e., race, ethnicity, poverty, gender) puts individuals at increased vulnerability to stressors (Barbarin et al., 2019). In recent years, much attention has been devoted to how educational settings have mirrored the same disparities in opportunities and bias for marginalized groups present in larger societies (Ladson-Billings, 2021). Educational research has supported this claim, even for our youngest students. According to the U.S. Department of Education Office of Civil Rights (2014), Black preschool children were three times more likely to be suspended or expelled compared to White students. Since this data were disseminated, researchers have attempted to determine the mechanism underlying this "discipline gap." As early as preschool, teachers were observed to track the movements of Black children, particularly Black males, at higher levels than White children (Gilliam et al., 2016). Children from marginalized groups (i.e., Black, Hispanic, poor) had more behavior complaints from early childhood teachers compared to non-poor White/Hispanic children, despite independent observations showing no differences among groups in disruptive behaviors (Sabol et al., 2022). Consistent with these findings, when male children were observed from kindergarten to first grade, teachers watched Black males more than White males and frequently punished the behaviors of Black males while ignoring the same behaviors in White males (Zimmermann, 2024). Black students in elementary schools were more likely to experience conflicts with their teachers, resulting in low quality relationships (Spilt & Hughes, 2015). These research results, among many others not discussed here, have supported that Black children's experiences in educational settings are different than other children.

Moreover, when Black children are treated differently in the classroom, other children are watching and actively making meaning of these discipline interactions (Meltzoff & Gilliam, 2024). Young children are developing the cognitive and social skills to interpret interactions with others and detect mistreatment and stereotypes. Children as young as three are knowledgeable about gender stereotypes and knowledgeable about racial stereotypes by age four or five (Brown & Bigler, 2005). In their developmental framework outlining how children perceive discrimination, Brown and Bigler (2005) have proposed that around the age of six, children have the social and cognitive skills to detect discrimination in many situations. Yet detecting discrimination might be possible at younger ages in blatant situations: if the child's social group is explicitly labeled and the person discriminating overtly states their beliefs. Similar to adults, children are more likely to detect discrimination and have more awareness of stereotypes that pertain to their social group (Brown & Bigler, 2004; McKown & Weinstein, 2003). Preschool children understood that excluding someone from an activity because of their race or gender was unfair (Theimer et al., 2001). In summary, not all children experience educational settings in the same manner, and furthermore, children recognize when they are being treated differently due to their race and/or gender.

Given young children are beginning to identify stereotypes and mistreatment in educational settings, how do young Black children make sense of these interactions? How do young Black children cope with mistreatment and discrimination? How does the discipline gap in early childhood classrooms impact young Black children's emerging sense of self? In the past, theories of child development were not created with these questions in mind. In a recent review of theories of child development (Saracho, 2023), only Bronfenbrenner's theory (Bronfenbrenner, 1979), which is focused on considering the contexts of child development, was included as an ecological theory that has impacted early childhood education.

In the current paper, we introduce another ecological theory of child development proposed to address the fallacy that children experience contexts equally: Phenomenological Variant of Ecological Systems theory (herein called Spencer's PVEST; Spencer et al., 1997; Spencer, 2006). Expanding on Bronfenbrenner's theory, Spencer argued that although children might develop in similar contexts, individual children experience contexts differently, particularly children from marginalized groups. Early childhood researchers cannot assume that children experience and interpret the same context (e.g., classroom) in the same way even when their behavior is the same. How young children mentally represent and interpret these experiences contributes to their developing sense of self.

For the current article, we have two main goals: 1) introduce Spencer's PVEST to the field of early childhood education, and 2) apply the components of this theory to young children's developing sense of self. Our review will be focused on research on Black children in early childhood and/or elementary educational settings (Spencer, 1982, Spencer et al., 1997).

Although this decision has constrained our review to only one group of children and one developmental outcome, it is simply to narrow the synthesis of the existing literature to address our two goals. Yet the overarching aim of our paper is to argue that Spencer's PVEST should be employed in early educational research to understand the unique experiences of children from marginalized groups, and how those unique experiences may impact young children's self-understanding. Spencer's PVEST has provided a theoretical framework to encourage investigations of how children make meaning of their experiences depending on their vulnerability (risk vs protective factors), stress level (challenges vs support), and coping strategies (adaptive vs maladaptive).

Introduction to Spencer's PVEST

Consistent with a long history of theoretical and empirical research on factors that influence children's risk and resilience (Fraser & Terzian, 2005; Rutter, 1979), Spencer's PVEST has proposed that risk and protective factors balance to determine an individual's net vulnerability. Net vulnerability pertains to individuals' predispositions or susceptibilities to stressors based on personal characteristics. Net vulnerability involves an individuals' self-appraisal processes related to their awareness of societal assumptions and biases, based on personal characteristics such as race, sex, socioeconomic status, to name a few (Cunningham et al, 2023; Spencer et al., 2012). With increasing age, children's more advanced cognitive and social skills mean that they may internalize societal biases and assumptions. Internalization of societal biases about personal characteristics become infused into children's developing sense of self. For children belonging to marginalized groups, internalization of bias and stereotypes, without the balance of protective factors such as supportive families and communities, influences their developing sense of self initially, and ultimately, their identity development as they approach adolescence.

Interacting with net vulnerabilities, Spencer has incorporated the notion of net vulnerabilities as having an impact on the perceived net stress, which refers to the cumulative impact of stressors that individuals encounter within their environments. The concept of net stress serves to recognize that stressors vary in intensity and frequency and have a collective effect on individuals' experiences. However, individuals encounter challenges within situations with varying levels of support to be able to face those challenges. When supports provided help individuals to offset the stressful impact of challenges, perceived net stress is reduced.

Facing challenges, either with or without supports, provides the foundation determining individuals' capacity to react to their environment. Using the concept of reactive coping processes, Spencer has highlighted how individuals respond to stressors using various coping mechanisms, which can be adaptive or maladaptive, based on their effectiveness. As highlighted by Spencer et al. (2012), in situations of net stress where challenges outweigh the supports available, individuals are more prone to adopt maladaptive strategies. Conversely, when supports outweigh the challenges, individuals can effectively adapt to and address challenges within different contexts. Including positive aspects in the model such as supports and adaptive coping, Spencer (2006) has provided a counternarrative to the overwhelming deficit view of children from marginalized backgrounds in the field of developmental psychology (Raver & Blair, 2020). Given the power of Spencer's PVEST to guide inquiries into the lived experiences of children from marginalized groups, both positive and negative, researchers have called for a broad application of her theory to lifespan development (Cunningham et al., 2023).

Young children's developing sense of self

Spencer's (1982) research with preschool children as well as her seminal work with marginalized adolescents (Spencer et al., 2015) has drawn on the lifespan theory of personality development of Erik Erikson (1950, 1959). Erikson proposed that children navigate different "crises" that are developmentally appropriate for their age. For the period of early childhood, crises involve 1) trust vs mistrust; 2) autonomy vs shame; 3) initiative vs guilt. Closely associated with the concept of attachment, Erikson argued that the first crisis involved children processing whether other people could be trusted. Children develop trust in others, particularly caregivers, when they perceive others as warm, responsive, and consistent. Due to the ability to trust others, children seek out and feel comforted by being around others and tend to experience tension and discomfort when separated from the trusted person (i.e., stranger anxiety). Within this same developmental time frame, by the age of 18-24 months, children gain a sense of self: the concept that they exist as a separate person, signaling a major milestone in self-understanding (Kärtner et al., 2012).

Once children understand that they exist separately from others, their growing cognitive skills help them to develop self-awareness, or the ability to describe and understand themselves. Increased self-awareness is developed within different contexts such as family and school, in social interactions where children are operating more independently from primary caregivers. When parents are supportive in letting children make age-appropriate decisions, children feel good about their growing autonomy and develop knowledge of their strengths and weaknesses. However, if children are severely punished or criticized for making age-appropriate choices, then they may develop doubts about their competence and/or shame about their behaviors.

With growing autonomy and competence, children begin to initiate their own actions based on the development of their conscience—the internalization of parental rules and standards—and feeling guilt when they break rules and fall short of parental expectations. When parents' reactions to their children's failure to meet their standards are warm and responsive, children will maintain their level of initiative to continue to pursue new goals. Yet if parents' reactions are highly controlling and/or overly punitive, children will experience guilt. When children experience overwhelming feelings of guilt based on these parental reactions, their initiative may suffer as they will worry about falling short of parental standards. Although Erikson focused on parents, early childhood teachers establishing trusting relationships with their children and their reactions to young children's growing independence also impact the development of children's trust, autonomy, and initiative.

Whereas Erikson's theory centered on children's struggles through developmentally appropriate challenges, Spencer's writings are focused on the environment as providing the necessary conditions for children to successfully navigate developmental challenges. She wrote, "When young children are deprived of opportunities to interact optimally within their environmental and social worlds, their transition into the next stage of development and nature of the constructed self may be compromised" (Spencer et al., 2015. p. 753). While the stages might be viewed as normative development processes that arise from similar developmental challenges, the contexts in which children navigate these crises vary dramatically (Brittian, 2012; Kroger, 2018; Maree, 2021). Moreover, children are influenced by their environments as well as they are influencing their environments (Brittian, 2012). According to Spencer et al. (2015), development of children and youth must be examined within the context of social and economic inequalities, as social messages about race and gender begin early in life and contribute to how contexts are experienced differently for children from marginalized backgrounds.

Spencer's PVEST and Early Childhood Education

Spencer's PVEST model introduced several crucial components that shed light on human development within ecological contexts that differ in social and economic conditions. Children's development of trust of others, autonomy, and initiative are closely connected to children's social and emotional learning. Using the conceptual model of Blewitt et al. (2020a) outlining the factors that support social and emotional learning within early childhood settings, we will overlay components of Blewitt et al. (2020a) with components of Spencer's PVEST: 1) net vulnerability with teacher attributes; 2) net stress with teacher-child relationships; and 3) reactive coping with strategies for social and emotional learning.

Net vulnerability and teacher attributes: Protective factors offset risk factors

Teachers play a critical role in the quality of learning interactions in the early childhood classroom that, in turn, have important implications for children's developmental outcomes (Burchinal et al., 2008; Hamre & Pianta, 2001; Mashburn et al., 2008). Teachers' capacity to create high quality learning experiences within a secure and nurturing climate in their classroom has been associated with their professional well-being (Cassidy et al., 2017) and their psychological well-being (Vesely et al., 2022). Within the PVEST model, protective factors for young children would include early childhood teachers' professional well-being (i.e., feelings about their work environment and perceptions of autonomy to make decisions) which have been related to positive outcomes such as job satisfaction and commitment to their profession (Bloom, 1996). Moreover, teachers' professional well-being impacts their ability to create high quality classroom environments (Dennis & O'Connor, 2013; Lower & Cassidy, 2007). Teachers' feelings about their work and autonomy in the workplace predicted higher scores on their ability to provide emotional support to toddlers within their classrooms (Cassidy et al., 2017). When teachers reported feeling a strong sense of community in their workplace, preschool children displayed less frustration and defiance in the classroom according to teachers' reports (Bostic et al., 2023). Moreover, when teachers reported higher levels of commitment to their teaching roles, they reported children as being less anxious/ withdrawn. Although teachers' work engagement did not moderate the relationship between teachers' sense of community and children's anger-aggression behaviors, when work engagement was added as a moderator, Black and Hispanic students had lower levels of reported anger-aggression (Bostic et al., 2023). Although these results are preliminary, they suggest that teachers' work engagement might help to reduce stereotypes of children of color as angry, reducing disproportionality in discipline rates between White and Black children (Gilliam et al., 2016).

Although many people have reported increased stress in the workplace, particularly following the pandemic, it is no exaggeration to say that teachers have been especially impacted. Early childhood teachers have reported high levels of stress and burnout given the demands of their job (Bullough et al., 2014; Cumming, 2017; Kwon et al., 2020). Teachers' burnout and turnover have negative impacts on children's development (Cassidy et al., 2011; Jeon & Ardeleanu, 2020). Early childhood teachers who perceived few supports and job resources were more likely to request children's expulsion (Zinsser et al., 2019). Given the racial disparities in discipline in elementary schools (Cipollone et al., 2022a), high levels of teachers' burnout within early childhood settings may represent a risk factor for young Black children.

In summary, reducing children of color's net vulnerability within early childhood settings will involve creating spaces for early childhood teachers to feel a sense of community and engagement within their workplace. When teachers felt supported in their workplace, they were better able to provide children with emotional support, and viewed their students as having fewer behavioral problems. When people are stressed, they have little time and energy to stop and reflect on their decisions and what may be influencing those decisions. As they say on every flight—adults are to put their mask on before they put on their children's mask. Teachers must experience optimal professional and psychological well-being through supportive workplace environments to create effective learning environments and establish high quality teacher-child relationships.

Net stress and quality of teacher-child relationships: Supports offset challenges

When teachers are working in supportive early childhood settings that support their well-being, teachers' stress is reduced. Teachers' stress is one of the attributes that influences teacher-child interactions involving instructional support, classroom organization, and emotional support. Moreover, there is a bidirectional relationship between these three types of teacher support and the quality of their relationships with children. When teachers were warm, sensitive, and responsive, their students were more likely to show positive adjustments to school (Blewitt et al., 2020a; Curby et al., 2009; Mashburn et al., 2009). In short, children who have close, emotional ties to their teachers benefit from feelings of safety and trust within teacher-child interactions (Hamre et al., 2008). Children who have close relationships with their teachers feel supported, reducing the stress levels within early childhood classrooms.

When children trust their teachers, they are more likely to explore their environment, leading to increases in children's autonomy. Research on the quality of teacher-child relationships has generally examined two dimensions: closeness and conflict. Closeness represents the amount of warmth and positive affect in the relationship, whereas conflict represents the amount of tension and anger in the relationship (Pianta & Nimetz, 1991). Moreover, high levels of conflict within teacher-child relationships have been associated with children's externalizing behaviors, and low levels of closeness in teacher-child relationships with children's internalizing behaviors (Howes, 2000; Jerome et al., 2009; Pianta & Nimetz, 1991). Teacher-child relationships have also been associated with academic success: teacher-child closeness predicted expressive vocabulary at the end of the school year (Cadima et al., 2019). Moreover, teachers' autonomy support (i.e., allowing for children to direct their interests and learning) predicted children's self-regulation at the end of the school year, even controlling for initial levels of self-regulation. One potential explanation for this finding is that when children had choices and felt a sense of autonomy, they selected more challenging activities, helping them to enhance their self-regulation skills (Cadima et al., 2019).

In addition to the construct of closeness, researchers have also used the term emotional support to examine teacher-child relationships, and teachers' emotional support predicted children's social and academic performance (Commodari, 2013; Howes, 2000). Teachers who used high levels of emotional support in their classrooms had students who scored higher on social competence, autonomy, and reduced problem behaviors (National Institute of Child Health and Human Development Early Child Care Research Network & Duncan, 2003; Mashburn et al., 2008). Emotionally supportive interactions with teachers might be particularly important for children who struggle with social and emotional development. When children with high levels of disruptive behaviors were observed to be emotionally secure in completing a task with their teacher, those children had higher ratings of task engagement compared to children that were not observed to be emotionally secure (Alamos & Williford, 2019). One dimension of teachers' emotional support that might be important is consistency. Children with lower levels of emotional regulation were more adjusted to preschool when their teachers were consistent in their use of emotional support, as opposed to the overall quantity of teachers' emotional support (Bailey et al., 2022).

In contrast, teachers who display lower levels of emotional support and/or autonomy support may present a challenging environment for young children, particularly children who struggle with emotional regulation. Children with lower levels of emotional regulation struggled more than their peers with higher levels of emotional regulation when teachers showed low levels of emotional support (Commodari, 2013; Bailey et al., 2016). In short, children with lower levels of emotional regulation and little support from teachers were left to rely on their own abilities to navigate classroom interactions (Bailey et al., 2016; Dominguez et al., 2011).

In summary, teachers who have close relationships and provide consistent emotional support, within activities that revolve around children's choices, offer an optimal setting for children to develop their autonomy. What remains a mystery, however, is how young children from marginalized groups form strong emotional connections with their teachers and the impact of these relationships on their learning and development. Empirical research with elementary teachers has suggested that Black children may struggle to connect with their teachers more than White children (Goldberg & Iruka, 2023). Teachers in public schools, 80% of whom are White (Institute for Education Sciences, National Center for Education Statistics [IES NCES], 2019), had more conflicts in their relationships with Black students compared to other students (Gallagher et al., 2013; Jerome et al., 2009). Teachers reported more conflicts with Black students compared to other students across the elementary school years, even after controlling for relevant child variables (Hajovsky et al., 2020; McKinnon & Blair, 2018; Murray & Murray, 2004; Redding, 2019; Spilt & Hughes, 2015). Black students also reported more conflicts with teachers compared to other students (Hughes et al., 2012; Murray et al., 2008).

Perhaps one potential explanation for these findings is a racial anger bias: prospective teachers were more like to rate Black boys and Black girls incorrectly as being angry compared to White boys and White girls (Halberstadt et al., 2022). Moreover, Black preschool boys have faced higher expulsion rates than other students, indicating that race contributes to the nature of teacher-child dynamics (Novak, 2023). According to the *Student Discipline and School Climate in U.S. Public Schools* report (United States Department of Education, 2023), Black public preschool children were suspended from school at nearly twice the rate of their enrollment in public preschools.

These results should serve as a caution for early childhood educational researchers: children's race/ethnicity must be examined in research on teacher-child relationships. Using Spencer's PVEST as a guiding framework, researchers must investigate teacher-child relationships within early childhood settings, with the assumption that children from marginalized groups may experience their classrooms differently than White children.

Reactive coping processes and social and emotional learning: Adaptive coping offsets maladaptive coping

According to Spencer's PVEST, net vulnerabilities feed into net stress: more protective factors reduce vulnerabilities and more supports reduce net stress, enabling resources that can be focused on devising adaptive coping strategies when challenges do arise. However, as we are considering young children, even under the best of circumstances, they may be limited in their abilities to devise adaptive coping strategies. Researchers have argued that adaptive coping strategies should be taught during the early school years, typically falling under the heading of social and emotional learning. Over the past few decades, researchers and educators have focused increasing attention on how children's social and emotional skills positively contribute to their approaches to learning and adjustment to school (Rademacher et al., 2021). The development of social and emotional skills is a normal process, involving acquiring and using knowledge related to understanding emotions in oneself and others, regulating emotions, and forming positive relationships with others (Collaborative for Academic, Social, and Emotional Learning [CASEL], 2021). Yet young children need guidance and support of adults as they navigate this developmental process. Early childhood settings might be children's first time engaged in extended interaction with other adults and peers of the same age, and teachers' guidance and coaching might be necessary. As such, early childhood teachers are important facilitators of the development of children's social and emotional skills. According to the conceptual model of Blewitt et al. (2020a), teachers that have established nurturing relationships with their children, and create supportive learning environments that cater to children's growing autonomy, will provide the optimal situation for most children to feel supported as they grapple with social and emotional learning.

However, like most traits, there are individual differences in children's social and emotional learning. Children who struggle with emotional regulation and social competence (i.e., engaging in effective interactions with others) will need more extensive support to develop adaptive ways to cope with their negative emotions and conflicts with others. Research on social and emotional learning (SEL) interventions in elementary schools have revealed that young children, particularly children who may struggle with emotional regulation, have benefited from additional curricula focused on social and emotional learning (Blewitt et al., 2020b; Daunic et al., 2023). Presumably, these benefits are related to helping students to develop adaptive ways of coping with stressful academic and social situations. However, it is equally plausible that these programs have bi-directional effects: as young children learn more appropriate ways to cope with academic and/or social challenges, their relationship with their teacher improves (McCormick et al., 2015).

Similar to school-age children, a variety of SEL programs have been created for use with preschool and kindergarten children in educational settings (Housman et al., 2023; Kramer et al., 2010), despite some cautions from the research (Moreno et al., 2019). Consistent with the research on teacher-child relationships, within these SEL programs, teachers learn that children develop social and emotional skills when they are embedded in safe and caring environments. Teachers are given strategies to approach misbehaviors as learning opportunities as opposed to punishments, within the context of caring relationships (Housman et al., 2023; Wilburn et al., 2023). In doing so, teacher training within SEL programs help teachers to support their students in learning adaptive coping strategies to approach and solve conflicts with teachers and peers.

When Head Start teachers used Conscious Discipline (CD; Bailey, 2014), an SEL program with these elements of teaching problem solving within a safe environment, their classrooms were rated as being "high quality" compared to teachers that did not use these techniques (Anderson et al., 2020). Moreover, teachers that consistently used CD had children who scored higher on measures of executive functioning (i.e., skills needed for self-regulation) and social skills, but not academic skills (Anderson et al., 2020). Additionally, when teachers consistently used CD, children in these classrooms had higher scores on social knowledge (i.e., self/ social awareness scale) that may have helped them to navigate relationships with peers and teachers. The combination of social knowledge and increased self-regulation may lead to positive reactive coping strategies, such as being able to inhibit negative behaviors and thinking about how to solve the conflict.

Whereas CD is rooted in attachment theory, another SEL program, Insights (O'Connor et al., 2014), is rooted in theories of temperament. The program provided teachers and parents with information about different types of children's temperament, and children were given situations in which to consider how they might interact with peers of different temperament types. Children learned adaptive coping strategies to deal with social interactions with peers that have emotional tendencies due to their temperaments (i.e., shy, angry). When researchers compared children in the Insights group with children in the control group, children in the Insights group had reduced problem behaviors (O'Connor et al., 2014), reduced off-task and disruptive behaviors (McCormick et al., 2015), increased behavioral engagement (McCormick et al., 2015) and greater academic gains (O'Connor et al, 2014) compared to children in the control group. Perhaps most importantly, the greatest effects of the Insights program were for children with severe behavioral problems, difficult temperaments, and male students (Iverson & Gartstein, 2018). Moreover, teacher-child relationships may have been the mediating factor; children with difficult temperaments in the Insights group had higher quality teacher-student relationships compared to children with difficult temperaments in the control group (McCormick et al., 2015).

Although only two SEL programs are reviewed here, numerous SEL programs are available for preschool and early elementary school (for a review of meta-analyses, see Durlak et al., 2022). Returning to Spencer's PVEST, a lingering question is how young children from marginalized backgrounds have responded to SEL techniques in their early childhood classrooms. One caution from researchers noted that SEL programs in public K-12 schools are not culturally neutral and, in fact, tend to have origins in White, middle-class norms of behavior (Robbins & Cipollone, 2023; Simmons, 2019). Moreover, Cipollone and colleagues (2022a) have suggested that SEL programs are forms of classroom management geared more toward controlling children, as opposed to truly aiding them in managing and experiencing their emotions. One major limitation of SEL research has been the failure to examine student characteristics such as race/ethnicity, disability status, and/or family income as potential moderating factors on SEL intervention outcomes (Cipriano et al., 2023a; Durlak et al., 2022).

Research on SEL program outcomes in early childhood settings must examine the effectiveness of these programs for different groups of children (Cipriano et al., 2023a, 2023b). One positive movement in education has been to examine SEL program components within an equity lens to determine how well these programs might meet the needs of children from diverse identities and cultures (Ramirez et al., 2021). To this end, CASEL, the leading research and advocacy center for SEL, recently embarked on a reimagining of their mission and core components, referred to as Transformative SEL (Jagars et al., 2021). With transformative SEL, CASEL has embraced the domains of identity, agency, belonging, collaborative problem solving, and curiosity as components of SEL programs. Transformative CASEL domains have conceptual overlap with the positive aspects of Spencer's PVEST (protective factors, support, and adaptive coping).

Spencer's PVEST: Using theory to inform early childhood research

For the current article, we had two main goals: 1) to introduce Spencer's PVEST to the field of early childhood education; and 2) to apply the components of this theory to young children's self-understanding. Spencer's PVEST offers a valuable framework for informing research in early childhood by providing a nuanced understanding of how children's subjective experiences interact with their environmental contexts. In the context of early childhood research, Spencer's PVEST can be used to investigate various factors influencing children's development, considering their vulnerabilities, stressors, and coping mechanisms within ecological systems.

In summarizing our application of Spencer's PVEST, the center of the model would include "normative human systemic processes" or typical developmental outcomes as young children's development of sense of self (trust, autonomy, initiative) and "individual at a specific developmental stage" as early childhood. The model represents the cumulative effects on developmental outcomes, hence "net," across different contexts (e.g., homes, schools, communities), with classrooms being one of those important contexts. For net vulnerabilities for young children in our society, some examples of risk factors include minority status and growing up in poverty. Yet protective factors such as increased representation of diverse teachers and positive messages, such as using books with diverse characters, may help buffer young children from the effects of these risk factors. Black preschoolers' initiative (i.e., choosing tasks independently) was higher when there was a racial match between both the assistant and lead teacher in Black majority preschools (Hong et al., 2023). Increasingly, early childhood educators are calling for classroom libraries that are more representative of racial and linguistic diversity and include positive portrayals (Naqvi et al., 2013).

Young children growing up in poverty experience what is considered a risk factor under net vulnerability, since families living in poverty encounter real-life challenges related to living in underfunded neighborhoods such as limited access to quality healthcare, recreational facilities, and safe environments (Gibson, 2015; Gomez et al., 2020; Weinberger, 2023). When families are stressed, children experience stress directly (e.g., limited food) and indirectly (e.g., parents working long hours). Challenges associated with living in poverty contribute to young children's net stress, tipping the balance toward increased stress. However, supportive factors are also present in the lives of young children. Researchers have advocated that equal attention should be allotted to the supports and strengths in neighborhoods, even those neighborhoods that might be classified as having families "living in poverty" (Cipollone et al., 2022b; Mims et al., 2023). Positive relationships with family members, friends, and trusted adults provide crucial emotional support and encouragement, supporting young children's developing sense of self. In the same way, teachers with close and emotionally supportive relationships with their children help to develop children's trust, autonomy, and initiative in classroom settings. Researchers can explore how young children from marginalized groups perceive and interpret stressors within their classrooms and how their interpretation impacts their developing sense of self.

With more research on how young children perceive and interpret stressors within classrooms, researchers can begin to explore children's spontaneous coping strategies and their effectiveness. Although early childhood educators have embraced teaching young children adaptive coping strategies as part of their curriculum, researchers have begun to question the appropriateness of some components of social and emotional curricula for all young children (Cipriano et al., 2023a; Durlak et al., 2022; Ramirez et al., 2021). More research is needed to observe how young children react to social and cognitive challenges in classroom settings. Spencer's PVEST can inform research on social and emotional learning in early childhood: understanding how different groups of children (e.g., minority, disability status, poverty) spontaneously react to challenges with adaptive coping can aid in identifying effective interventions and support systems. Research using this framework can shed light on how supportive environments and relevant social and emotional learning curriculum influence the development of trust, autonomy, and initiative in young children.

Spencer's PVEST provides a valuable framework for understanding how young children perceive and construct their self-awareness within their environmental contexts. Over time, young children's developing sense of self, either positive (trust, autonomy, and initiative) or negative (mistrust, shame, guilt) evolves into their more stable, emerging identities in middle childhood and adolescence. Setting the stage for the development of children's positive emerging identities involves educational spaces with teachers that can create secure and welcoming places, along with challenging activities to support young children's developing cognitive and social skills.

References

Alamos, P., & Williford, A. P. (2019). Exploring dyadic teacher-child interactions, emotional security, and task engagement in preschool children displaying externalizing behaviors. *Social Development, 29*(1), 339-355. https://doi.org/10.1111/sode.12403

Anderson, K. L., Weimer, M., & Fuhs, M. W. (2020). Teacher fidelity to CD and children's executive function skills. *Early Childhood Research Quarterly, 51*, 14–25. https://doi.org/10.1016/j.ecresq.2019.08.003

Bailey, B. A. (2014). *Conscious Discipline: Building resilient classrooms*. Loving Guidance.

Bailey, C. S., Denham, S. A., Curby, T. W., & Bassett, H. H. (2016). Emotional and organizational supports for preschoolers' emotion regulation: Relations with school adjustment. *Emotion, 16*(2), 263–279. DOI: 10.1037/a0039772

Bailey, C. S., Ondrusek, A. R., Curby, T. W., & Denham, S. A. (2022). Teachers' consistency of emotional support moderates the association between young children's regulation capacities and their preschool adjustment. *Psychology in the Schools, 59*, 1051-1074. https://doi.org/10.1002/pits.22659

Barbarin, O. A., Hitti, A., & Copeland-Linder, N. (2019). Behavioral and emotional development of African American boys growing up in risky environments. *Child Development Perspectives, 13*(4), 215-220. https://doi.org/10.1111/cdep.12341

Blewitt, C., Morris, H., Nolan, A., Jackson, K., Barrett, H., & Skouteris, H. (2020a). Strengthening the quality of educator-child interactions in early childhood education and care settings: a conceptual model to improve mental health outcomes for preschoolers. *Early Child Development and Care, 190*(7), 991-1004. https://doi.org/10.1080/03004430.2018.1507028

Blewitt, C., O'Connor, A., Morris, H., Mousa, A., Bergmeier, H., Nolan, A., Jackson, K., Barrett, H., & Skouteris H. (2020b). Do curriculum-based social and emotional learning programs in early childhood education and care strengthen teacher outcomes? A systematic literature review. *International Journal of Environmental Research and Public Health, 17*(3), 1049. https://doi.org/10.3390/ijerph17031049

Bloom, P. (1996). The quality of work life in NAEYC accredited and nonaccredited early childhood programs. *Early Education and Development, 7*, 301–317.

Bostic, B., Schock, N., Jeon, L., & Buettner, C. K. (2023). Early childhood teachers' sense of community and work engagement: Associations with children's social, emotional, and behavioral functioning. *Journal of School Psychology, 98*, 133–147. https://doi.org/10.1016/j.jsp.2023.02.007

Brittian, A. S. (2012). Understanding African American adolescents' identity development: A relational developmental systems perspective. *The Journal of Black Psychology, 38*(2), 172–200. https://doi.org/10.1177/0095798411414570

Bronfenbrenner, U. (1979). *The ecology of human development: Experiments by nature and design*. Cambridge, MA: Harvard University Press.

Brown, C. S., & Bigler, R. S. (2004). Children's perceptions of gender discrimination. *Developmental Psychology, 40*(5), 714–726. https://doi.org/10.1037/0012-1649.40.5.714

Brown, C. S., & Bigler, R. S. (2005). Children's perceptions of discrimination: A developmental model. *Child Development, 76*(3), 533-553. https://doi.org/10.1111/j.1467-8624.2005.00862.x

Bullough, R. V., Jr., Hall-Kenyon, K. M., MacKay, K. L., & Marshall, E. E. (2014). Head Start and the intensification of teaching in early childhood education. *Teaching and Teacher Education, 37,* 55-63. https://doi.org/10.1016/j.tate.2013.09.006

Burchinal, M., Howes, C., Pianta, R., Bryant, D., Early, D., Clifford, R., & Barbarin, O. (2008). Predicting child outcomes at the end of kindergarten from the quality of pre-kindergarten teacher-child interactions and instruction. *Applied Developmental Science, 12*(3), 140–153. https://doi.org/10.1080/10888690802199418

Cadima, J., Barros, S., Ferreira, T., Serra-Lemos, M., Leal, T., & Verschueren, K. (2019). Bidirectional associations between vocabulary and self-regulation in preschool and their interplay with teacher–child closeness and autonomy support, *Early Childhood Research Quarterly, 46,* 75-86. https://doi.org/10.1016/j.ecresq.2018.04.004.

Cassidy, D. J., King, E. K., Wang, Y. C., Lower, J. K., & Kintner-Duffy, V. L. (2017). Teacher work environments are toddler learning environments: Teacher professional well-being, classroom emotional support, and toddlers' emotional expressions and behaviours. *Early Child Development and Care, 187*(11), 1666. https://doi.org/10.1080/03004430.2016.1180516

Cassidy, D. J., Lower, J. K., Kintner-Duffy, V. L., Hegde, A. V., & Shim, J. (2011). The day-to-day reality of teacher turnover in preschool classrooms: An analysis of classroom context and teacher, director, and parent perspectives. *Journal of Research in Childhood Education, 25*(1), 1. https://doi.org/10.1080/02568543.2011.533118

Cipollone, K. Hoffman, E.B., & Sciuchetti, M. B. (2022a). Compliance and control: The hidden curriculum of social-emotional learning. *Perspectives on Early Childhood Psychology and Education, 6*(1). https://doi.org/10.58948/2834-8257.1005

Cipollone, K., Zygmunt, E., Scaife, R., & Scaife, W. (2022b). "Let's create the table": Reengaging democracy in teacher preparation through radical reciprocity. *Teachers College Record, 124*(3), 61–88. https://doi-org.proxy.bsu.edu/10.1177/01614681221086775

Cipriano, C., Naples, L. H., Eveleigh, A., Cook, A., Funaro, M., Cassidy, C., & Rappolt Schlichtmann, G. (2023a). A systematic review of student disability and race representation in universal school-based social and emotional learning interventions for elementary school students. *Review of Educational Research, 93*(1), 73-102. https://doi.org/10.3102/00346543221094079

Cipriano, C., Strambler, M. J., Naples, L. H., Ha, C., Kirk, M., Wood, M., Sehgal, K., Zieher, A. K., Eveleigh, A., McCarthy, M., Funaro, M., Ponnock, A., Chow, J. C., & Durlak, J. (2023b). The state of evidence for social and emotional learning: A contemporary meta- analysis of universal school-based SEL interventions. *Child Development, 94*(5), 1181- 1204. https://doi.org/10.1111/cdev.13968

Collaborative for Academic, Social, and Emotional Learning. (2021). *SEL: What are the core competence areas and where are they promoted?* https://casel.org/sel-framework/

Commodari, E. (2013). Preschool teacher attachment, school readiness and risk of learning difficulties. *Early Childhood Research Quarterly, 28*(1), 123–133. https://doi.org/10.1016/j.ecresq.2012.03.004

Cumming, T. (2017). Early childhood educators' well-being: An updated review of the literature. *Early Childhood Education Journal, 45*(5), 583–593. https://doi.org/10.1007/s10643-016-0818-6

Cunningham, M., Swanson, D. P., Youngblood, J., Seaton, E. K., Francois, S., & Ashford, C. (2023). Spencer's phenomenological variant of ecological systems theory (PVEST): Charting its origin and impact. *The American Psychologist, 78*(4), 524-534. https://doi.org/10.1037/amp0001051

Curby, T. W., Rimm-Kaufman, S. E., & Ponitz, C. C. (2009). Teacher-child interactions and children's achievement trajectories across kindergarten and first grade. *Journal of Educational Psychology, 101*(4), 912–925. https://doi.org/10.1037/a0016647

Daunic, A. P., Aydin, B., Corbett, N. L., Smith, S. W., Boss, D., & Crews, E. (2023). Social- emotional learning intervention for K–1 students at risk for emotional and behavioral disorders: Mediation effects of social-emotional learning on school adjustment. *Behavioral Disorders, 49*(1), 17-30. https://doi.org/10.1177/01987429231185098

Dennis, S. E., & O'Connor, E. (2013). Reexamining quality in early childhood education: Exploring the relationship between the organizational climate and the classroom. *Journal of Research in Childhood Education, 27*(1), 74–92. https://doi.org/10.1080/02568543.2012.739589

Domínguez, X., Vitiello, V. E., Fuccillo, J. M., Greenfield, D. B., & Bulotsky-Shearer, R. J. (2011). The role of context in preschool learning: A multilevel examination of the contribution of context-specific problem behaviors and classroom process quality to low-income children's approaches to learning. *Journal of School Psychology, 49*(2), 175–195. https://doi.org/10.1016/j.jsp.2010.11.002

Durlak, J. A., Mahoney, J. L., & Boyle, A. E. (2022). What we know, and what we need to find out about universal, school-based social and emotional learning programs for children and adolescents: A review of meta-analyses and directions for future research. *Psychological Bulletin, 148*(11–12), 765–782. https://doi.org/10.1037/bul0000383

Erikson, E. (1950). *Childhood and society*. New York: Norton.
Erikson, E. (1959). Identity and the life cycle. *Psychological Issues, 1*, 1–17.
Fraser, M. W., & Terzian, M. A. (2005). Risk and resilience in child development: Practice principles and strategies. In G. P. Mallon & P. McCartt Hess (Eds.), Handbook of children, youth, and family services: Practice, policies, and programs (pp. 55–71). New York: Columbia University Press.
Gallagher, K. C., Kainz, K., Vernon-Feagans, L., & White, K. M. (2013). Development of student–teacher relationships in rural early elementary classrooms. *Early Childhood Research Quarterly, 28*(3), 520–528. https://doi.org/10.1016/j.ecresq.2013.03.002
Gibson, G. A. (2015). Education vs schooling: Black adolescent females fight for an education in the 21st century. In C. F. Collins (Ed.), *Black girls and adolescents: Facing the challenges.* (pp. 199–210). Praeger/ABC-CLIO.
Gilliam, W., Maupin, A., Chin, R., Accavitti, M., & Shic, F. (2016). *Do early educators' implicit biases regarding sex and race relate to behavior expectations and recommendations of preschool expulsions and suspensions?* Yale University Child Study Center. https://medicine.yale.edu/childstudy/zigler/publications/Preschool%20 Implicit%20Bias%20Policy%20Brief_final_9_26_276766_5379_v1.pdf
Goldberg, M. J., & Iruka, I. U. (2023). The role of teacher–child relationship quality in Black and Latino boys' positive development. *Early Childhood Education Journal, 51*(2), 301–315. https://doi-org.proxy.bsu.edu/10.1007/s10643-021-01300-3
Gomez, S. F., Marshall, C., Jackson, R., & Allen, A. (2020). The portrait project: Content and process of identity development among young men of color in East Oakland. *Journal of Adolescent Research, 35*(3), 341–367. https://doi-org.proxy.bsu.edu/10.1177/0743558420908801
Hajovsky, D. B., Chesnut, S. R., & Jensen, K. M. (2020). The role of teachers' self-efficacy beliefs in the development of teacher-student relationships. *Journal of School Psychology, 82*, 141–158. https://doi-org.proxy.bsu.edu/10.1016/j.jsp.2020.09.001
Halberstadt, A. G., Cooke, A. N., Garner, P. W., Hughes, S. A., Oertwig, D., & Neupert, S. D. (2022). Racialized emotion recognition accuracy and anger bias of children's faces. *Emotion, 22*(3), 403–417. https://doi.org/10.1037/emo0000756
Hamre, B. K., & Pianta, R. C. (2001). Early teacher-child relationships and the trajectory of children's school outcomes through eighth grade. *Child Development, 72*(2), 625–638. https://doi.org/10.1111/1467-8624.00301
Hamre, B. K., Pianta, R. C., Downer, J. T., & Mashburn, A. J. (2008). Teachers' perceptions of conflict with young students: Looking beyond problem behaviors. *Social Development, 17*(1), 115–136. https://doi.org/10.1111/j.1467-9507.2007.00418.x
Hong, S. L., Legette, K. B., Kuhn, L., Zgourou, E., Kainz, K., Yazejian, N., & Iruka, I. U. (2023). Lead teacher, assistant teacher, and peer racial/ethnic match and child outcomes for black children enrolled in enhanced high-quality early care and education programs.
Early Childhood Research Quarterly, 64, 186-198. https://doi.org/10.1016/j. ecresq.2023.03.001

Housman, D. K., Cabral, H., Aniskovich, K., & Denham, S. A. (2023). The impact of "Begin to ECSEL" on children's self-regulation, executive functions and learning. *Early Child Development and Care, 193*(2), 159-173. https://doi.org/10.1080/03004430.2022.2071869

Howes, C. (2000). Social-emotional classroom climate in child care, child-teacher relationships and children's second grade peer relations. *Social Development, 9*(2), 191–204. https://doi.org/10.1111/1467-9507.00119

Hughes, J. N., Wu, J.-Y., Kwok, O., Villarreal, V., & Johnson, A. Y. (2012). Indirect effects of child reports of teacher–student relationship on achievement. *Journal of Educational Psychology, 104*(2), 350–365. https://doi-org.proxy.bsu.edu/10.1037/a0026339

Institute of Education Science, National Center for Education Statistics (2019). The Condition of Education. United States Department of Education. https://files.eric.ed.gov/fulltext/ED594978.pdf

Iverson, S. L., & Gartstein, M. A. (2018). Applications of temperament: A review of caregiver- focused temperament-driven interventions. *Early Education and Development 29*(1), 31–52. https://doi.org/10.1080/10409289.2017.1341805

Jagars, R. J., Skoog-Hoffman, A., Barthelus, B., & Schlund, J. (2021). Transformative social and emotional learning in pursuit of educational equity and excellence. *American Educator*, 12-17.

Jeon, L., & Ardeleanu, K. (2020). Work climate in early care and education and teachers' stress: Indirect associations through emotion regulation. *Early Education and Development, 31*(7), 1031–1051. https://doi.org/10.1080/10409289.2020.1776809

Jerome, E. M., Hamre, B. K., & Pianta, R. C. (2009). Teacher—child relationships from kindergarten to sixth grade: Early childhood predictors of teacher-perceived conflict and closeness. *Social Development, 18*(4), 915–945. https://doi.org/10.1111/sode.2009.18.issue-410.1111/j.1467-9507.2008.00508.x

Kärtner, J., Keller, H., Chaudhary, N., & Yovsi, R. D. (2012). The development of mirror self- recognition in different sociocultural contexts. *Monographs of the Society for Research in Child Development, 77*(4), vii–87. https://doi.org/10.1111/j.1540-5834.2012.00688.x

Kramer, T.J., Caldarella, P., Christensen, L., & Shatzer, R.H. (2010). Social and emotional learning in the kindergarten classroom: Evaluation of the Strong Start Curriculum. *Early Childhood Education Journal, 37*, 303-309.

Kroger, J. (2018). The epigenesis of identity- What does it mean? *Identity, 18*(4), 334. https://doi.org/10.1080/15283488.2018.1523730

Kwon, K. A., Ford, T. G., Salvatore, A. L., Randall, K., Jeon, L., Malek-Lasater, A., Ellis, N., Kile, M. S., Horm, D. M., Kim, S. G., & Han, M. (2020). Neglected elements of a high- quality early childhood workforce: Whole teacher well-being and working conditions. *Early Childhood Education Journal, 50*, 157–168. https://doi.org/10.1007/s10643-020-01124-7.

Ladson-Billings, G. (2021). I'm here for the hard re-set: Post pandemic pedagogy to preserve our culture. *Equity & Excellence in Education, 54*(1), 68-78. https://doi.org/10.1080/10665684.2020.1863883

Lower, J. K., & Cassidy, D. J. (2007). Child care work environments: The relationship with learning environments. *Journal of Research in Childhood Education, 22*(2), 189. https://doi.org/10.1080/02568540709594621

Maree, J. G. (2021). The psychosocial development theory of Erik Erikson: Critical overview. *Early Child Development and Care, 191*(7–8), 1107. https://doi.org/10.1080/03004430.2020.1845163

Mashburn, A. J., Justice, L. M., Downer, J. T., & Pianta, R. C. (2009). Peer effects on children's language achievement during pre-kindergarten. *Child Development, 80*(3), 686–702. https://doi.org/10.1111/j.1467-8624.2009.01291.x

Mashburn, A. J., Pianta, R. C., Hamre,, B. K., Downer J. T., Barbarin, O. A., Bryant, D., Burchinal, M., Early, D. M., & Howes, C. (2008). Measures of classroom quality in prekindergarten and children's development of academic, language, and social skills. *Child Development, 79*(3), 732-49. https://doi.org/10.1111/j.1467-8624.2008.01154.x

McCormick, M.P., O'Connor, E.E., Cappella, E., & McClowry, S.G. (2015). Getting a good start in school: Effects of INSIGHTS on children with high maintenance temperaments. *Early Childhood Research Quarterly, 30*, 128-139.

McKinnon, R. D., & Blair, C. (2018). Does early executive function predict teacher–child relationships from kindergarten to second grade? *Developmental Psychology, 54*(11), 2053–2066. https://doi-org.proxy.bsu.edu/10.1037/dev0000584

McKown, C., & Weinstein, R. S. (2003). The development and consequences of stereotype consciousness in middle childhood. *Child Development, 74*(2), 498-515. https://doi.org/10.1111/1467-8624.7402012

Meltzoff, A. N., & Gilliam, W. S. (2024). Young children & implicit racial biases. *Daedalus, 153*(1), 65-83. https://doi.org/10.1162/daed_a_02049

Mims, L., Bocknek, E., Duane, A., Hill, L., McGoron, L., & Stokes, K. (2023). "Coming together educationally creates a bond like no other": Exploring how families engage in black history home learning. *Journal of Black Psychology, 50*(2), 194-210. https://doi.org/10.1177/00957984231221035

Moreno, A. J., Nagasawa, M. K., & Schwartz, T. (2019). Social and emotional learning and early childhood education: Redundant terms? *Contemporary Issues in Early Childhood, 20*(3), 221-235.

Murray, C., & Murray, K. M. (2004). Child level correlates of teacher-student relationships: An examination of demographic characteristics, academic orientations, and behavioral orientations. *Psychology in the Schools, 41*(7), 751–762. https://doi-org.proxy.bsu.edu/10.1002/pits.20015

Murray, C., Murray, K. M., & Waas, G. A. (2008). Child and teacher reports of teacher-student relationships: Concordance of perspectives and associations with school adjustment in urban kindergarten classrooms. *Journal of Applied Developmental Psychology, 29*(1), 49–61. https://doi-org.proxy.bsu.edu/10.1016/j.appdev.2007.10.006

National Institute of Child Health and Human Development Early Child Care Research Network & Duncan, G. J. (2003). Modeling the impacts of child care quality on children's preschool cognitive development. *Child Development, 74*(5), 1454-1475. https://doi.org/10.1111/1467-8624.00617

Naqvi, R., McKeough, A., Thorne, K., & Pfitscher, C. (2013). Dual-language books as an emergent-literacy resource: Culturally and linguistically responsive teaching and learning. *Journal of Early Childhood Literacy, 13*(4), 501–528. https://doi- org.proxy.bsu.edu/10.1177/1468798412442886

Novak, S. (2023, January 12). Half of the 250 kids expelled from preschool each day are black boys. *Scientific American.* https://www.scientificamerican.com/article/half-of-the-250-kids-expelled-from-preschool-each-day-are-black-boys/

O'Connor, E. E., Cappella, E., McCormick, M. P., & McClowry, S. G. (2014). An examination of the efficacy of INSIGHTS in enhancing the academic and behavioral development of children in early grades. *Journal of Educational Psychology, 106*(4), 1156–1169. https://doi.org/10.1037/a0036615.

Pianta, R. C., & Nimetz, S. L. (1991). Relationships between children and teachers: Associations with classroom and home behavior. *Journal of Applied Developmental Psychology, 12*(3), 379–393. https://doi.org/10.1016/0193-3973(91)90007-Q

Rademacher, A., Goagoses, N., Schmidt, S., Zumbach, J., & Koglin, U. (2021). Preschoolers' profiles of self-regulation, social-emotional and behavior skills and its prediction for a successful behavior adaptation during the transitional period from preschool to elementary school. *Early Education and Development, 17*(4), 1–15. https://doi.org/10.1080/10409289.2021.1958283

Ramirez, T., Brush, K., Raisch, N., Bailey, R., & Jones, S.M. (2021). Equity in social emotional learning programs: A content analysis of equitable practices in PreK-5 SEL programs. *Frontiers in Education, 6*:679467. https://doi.org/10.3389/feduc.2021.679467

Raver, C. C., & Blair, C. (2020). Developmental science aimed at reducing inequality: Maximizing the social impact of research on executive function in context. *Infant and Child Development, 29*(1), n/a-n/a. https://doi.org/10.1002/icd.2175

Redding, C. (2019). A teacher like me: A review of the effect of student–teacher racial/ethnic matching on teacher perceptions of students and student academic and behavioral outcomes. *Review of Educational Research, 89*(4), 499-535. https://doi.org/10.3102/0034654319853545

Robbins, K., & Cipollone, K. (2023) The real learning loss: A lost opportunity to reimagine schooling, *Educational Studies, 59*(2), 184-205. https://doi.org/10.1080/00131946.2023.2169695

Rutter, M. (1979). Protective factors in children's responses to stress and disadvantage. In M. W. Kent & J. E. Rolf (Eds.), *Primary prevention of psychopathology: Vol. 3. Social competence in children* (pp. 49–74). University Press of New England.

Sabol, T. J., Kessler, C. L., Rogers, L. O., Petitclerc, A., Silver, J., Briggs-Gowan, M., & Wakschlag, L. S. (2022). A window into racial and socioeconomic status disparities in preschool disciplinary action using developmental methodology. *Annals of the New York Academy of Sciences, 1508*(1), 123-136. https://doi.org/10.1111/nyas.14687

Saracho, O. N. (2023). Theories of child development and their impact on early childhood education and care. *Early Childhood Education Journal, 51*, 15-30. https://doi.org/10.1007/s10643-021-01271-5

Simmons, D. (2019, April). Why we can't afford whitewashed social-emotional learning. *ASCD, 61*(4), 2-3. Retrieved from https://www.ascd.org/el/articles/why-we-cant-afford-whitewashedsocial-emotional-learning.

Spencer, M. B. (1982). Preschool children's social cognition and cultural cognition: A cognitive developmental interpretation of race dissonance findings. *Journal of Psychology, 112*(2), 275-286.

Spencer, M. B. (2006). Phenomenology and ecological systems theory: Development of diverse groups. In R. M. Lerner & W. Damon (Eds.), *Handbook of child psychology: Theoretical models of human development* (6th ed., pp. 829–893). John Wiley & Sons, Inc.

Spencer, M. B., Dupree, D., & Hartmann, T. (1997). A phenomenological variant of ecological systems theory (PVEST): A self-organization perspective in context. *Development and Psychopathology, 9*(4), 817. https://doi.org/10.1017/S0954579497001454

Spencer, M. B., Dupree, D., Tinsley, B., McGee, E. O., Hall, J., Fegley, S. G., & Elmore, T. G. (2012). Resistance and resiliency in a color-conscious society: Implications for learning and teaching. In S. Graham, T. Urdan, C. B. McCormick, K. R. Harris, J. Sweller & G. M. Sinatra (Eds.), *APA Educational Psychology Handbook*, Theories, constructs, and critical issues (pp. 461-494). American Psychological Association. https://doi.org/10.1037/13273-016

Spencer, M. B., Swanson, D. P., & Harpalani, V. (2015). Development of the self. In R.M. Lerner & M.E. Lamb (Eds.), *Handbook of Child Psychology and Developmental Science, Vol. 3: Socioemotional processes*, 7th edition (p. 750 - 793). Wiley.

Spilt, J. L., & Hughes, J. N. (2015). African American children at risk of increasingly conflicted teacher–student relationships in elementary school. *School Psychology Review, 44*(3), 306–314. https://doi-org.proxy.bsu.edu/10.17105/spr-14-0033.1

Theimer, C. E., Killen, M., & Stangor, C. (2001). Young children's evaluations of exclusion in gender-stereotypic peer contexts. *Developmental Psychology., 37*(1), 18–27. https://doi.org/10.1037/0012-1649.37.1.18

United States Department of Education, Office for Civil Rights. (2014). Civil Rights Data Collection: Data Snapshot (School Discipline). Accessed August 4, 2021. https://ocrdata.ed.gov/Downloads/CRDC-School-Discipline-Snapshot.pdf.

United States Department of Education (November 2023), Office for Civil Rights, 2020-21 Civil Rights Data Collection. https://civilrightsdata.ed.gov.

Vesely, C. K., Brown, E. L., Mehta, S. & Horner, C. G. (2022). 'Staying Afloat': A mixed methods study of the financial and psychological well-being of early childhood educators. *Early Childhood Education Journal, 52,* 293–304. https://doi.org/10.1007/s10643-022-01429-9

Weinberger, E. C. (2023). Developmental trajectories of conduct problems across racial/ethnic identity and neighborhood context: A systematic review. *Aggression and Violent Behavior, 71,* 101844 https://doi.org/10.1016/j.avb.2023.101844.

Wilburn, E., John, S., Edge, N., Sutton, M., & Hickman, K. (2023). Examining the implementation of conscious discipline: A qualitative study utilizing the I-PARIHS framework. *Early Childhood Education Journal, 51,* 1131-1143.

Zimmermann, C. R. (2024). Looking for trouble: How teachers' racialized practices perpetuate discipline inequities in early childhood. *Sociology of Education, 97*(3), 219-232. https://doi.org/10.1177/00380407241228581

Zinsser, K. M., Zulauf, C. A., Das, V. N., & Silver, H. C. (2019). Utilizing social-emotional learning supports to address teacher stress and preschool expulsion. *Journal of Applied Developmental Psychology, 61,* 33–42. https://doi.org/10.1016/j.appdev.2017.11.006

An Equity-Based and Culturally Responsive Bill of Rights for Early Childhood Students of Color with Exceptionalities

Evette Simmons-Reed, Michelle Frazier Trotman Scott, Gloria Taradash, Mildred Boveda, and Donna Y. Ford

Abstract

The COVID-19 pandemic exacerbated existing disparities in Early Intervention (EI) and Early Childhood Special Education (ECSE) services for culturally and linguistically diverse (CLD) disabled children, exposing critical gaps in access, services and support. Systemic inconsistencies in implementation, training, and funding, remain barriers that limit opportunities for CLD students to benefit, despite the aims of the Individuals with Disabilities Improvement Act (IDEA). To address these inequities, this article proposes an expanded and updated Culturally Responsive Equity-Based Bill of Rights for EI and ECSE. Building upon Ford and colleagues' (2018) work, this revised document extends protections to children aged zero to five, emphasizing access to technology, internet, and healing-centered engagement services. It serves as a practical tool for parents, communities, schools, curriculum developers, and universities to advocate for and implement culturally sustaining practices. By highlighting the limitations of current legal frameworks and providing actionable recommendations, such as increased funding for culturally responsive training, this Bill of Rights aims to ensure equitable, culturally responsive education for all CLD disabled children, fostering improved outcomes and well-being.

Keywords: *early childhood special education, intervention, COVID-19, culturally responsive, disability*

The COVID-19 pandemic profoundly impacted education, especially early intervention (EI) and early childhood special education (ECSE) services for disabled children of color. The National

Institute of Early Education Research (NIEER) highlighted persistent state-by-state disparities in services based on race, ethnicity, gender, and socioeconomic status, contributing to unequal outcomes (Freidman & Barnett, 2023). These inequities limit academic progress for disabled students of color, potentially leading to trauma and harsh disciplinary actions, resulting in poorer outcomes.

Recognizing the urgent need to address these disparities, the authors of this article have expanded and updated Ford and colleague's bill of rights, originally focused on gifted students of color, to create a *Culturally Responsive Equity-Based Bill of Rights* for EI and ECSE (Ford et al., 2018). This, building on the 2018 work, now includes younger children aged zero to five. It emphasizes access to the internet, technology, and healing-centered engagement services as fundamental rights for students and families. Despite legal protections, disabled students of color often receive a public education that is technically free, but not appropriate as it relates to cultural responsiveness, due to systemic inequities. This Bill of Rights aims to fill that gap.

The *Bill of Rights for Early Childhood Students of Color with Exceptionalities* serves various stakeholders, including parents, communities, schools, curriculum developers, and universities. Parents and communities can use it to advocate for their children, while school districts can adopt it as a template for creating or revising policies and procedures for culturally sustaining services. Publishers and educators can integrate its principles into curriculum development, ensuring content is culturally relevant and rigorous. University faculty can use it to prepare future teachers and school psychologists with culturally responsive strategies, promoting students' healthy development and well-being. Before presenting the expanded equity based Bill of Rights, it is critical to understand the urgent context that necessitates such a framework. The following section will therefore provide a brief overview of the exacerbating impact of the COVID-19 pandemic on the education of disabled students of color.

Impact of COVID-19

The COVID-19 pandemic had a profound impact on all aspects of children's education, including early childhood program enrollment, student learning, and the educators that support them. Pre-K and elementary students, especially those with disabilities, experienced significant declines in enrollment and learning (Maier et al., 2021). This trend persisted beyond the initial stages of the pandemic, affecting children at a critical time for cognitive, linguistic, motor, and socio- emotional development.

The 2023 *State(s) of Early Intervention and Early Childhood Special Education: Looking at Equity* report from NIEER highlighted these shifts, noting a 15% decrease in Fall 2020 for IDEA Part C Early Intervention and a 16% decrease for IDEA Part B Early Childhood Special Education services compared to the previous year (Freidman-Krauss & Barnett, 2023). These reductions were widespread across states, emphasizing the pandemics profound impact on early intervention and early childhood education programs and the negative implications for learning and development.

Student enrollment and learning experiences during the pandemic were influenced by factors such as race/ethnicity, language, family income, and disability status. Marginalized groups experienced larger enrollment drops, with preschool attendance at 35% for children from families earning less than $25,000 compared to 48% for those from higher-income households (Friedman-Krauss & Barnett, 2023). The pandemic disrupted the provisions of IDEA, affecting children's access to Free and Appropriate Public Education (FAPE) and services in their Least Restrictive Environment (LRE), resulting in fewer services being delivered alongside their peers.

Disparities in literacy and math proficiency have persisted with Black, Hispanic, and Native American or Alaskan Native children showing lower progress compared to their White counterparts (National Center for Education Statistics [NCES], 2021). The pandemic exacerbated these disparities, especially affecting Black children and families receiving Early Childhood Special Education (ECSE) services.

While ECSE receipt decreased by 16% nationally between Fall 2019 and Fall 2020, the decrease was more pronounced for Black children (23%) than White children (18%). However, the decrease in receiving ECSE in inclusive settings was similar across racial/ethnic groups. Black children receiving EI also experienced a larger decrease in receiving services in community-based settings compared to children of other races (NCES, 2021).

Fear of the virus prompted many parents to opt for alternative service delivery modes, increasing services provided at home, in separate classes, or in-service provider locations for children with disabilities (Sullivan, 2021). Infants and toddlers were more likely to receive EI services at home after the pandemic began, indicating a shift in service delivery settings.

Many households, particularly families of color, encountered substantial hurdles in creating a learning environment comparable to that of school. While most low– and moderate– income families had some internet access, many were under-connected, relying solely on mobile devices with inconsistent connectivity. While discounted Internet services expanded during the pandemic, they have not reached all students in need (Mitchell, 2020).

Consequently, Black and Latino students were more likely to bear a disproportionate burden of learning loss. These disparities were further compounded by existing policies that already allocate fewer and lower-quality resources to students of color. These policies result in significantly larger class sizes, less qualified and experienced teachers, and limited access to high-quality curricula for Black and Latino students (Mitchell, 2020). Many parents felt ill-equipped to engage their younger children in remote learning, with almost half of those with preschool-aged children feeling overwhelmed by remote or hybrid instruction. Disruptions in their routine and environment lead to a sharp increase in behavioral issues among children.

The ongoing staffing difficulties and lower wages in early childhood education have significant implications for disabled children of color requiring EI and ECSE services, hindering recovery efforts. Educators faced similar difficulties, including operational stability, fluctuating enrollments, and health concerns, leading to reduced hours and higher turnover rates among early childhood educators compared to public school teachers. Addressing these challenges requires comprehensive support for children, families, and educators to mitigate the long-term impact of the pandemic on early childhood education.

Systemic Inequities in Education Affecting Disabled Children of Color Before and After the Pandemic

The pandemic exacerbated existing deep inequities experienced by children of color and their families due to discriminatory policies and institutional practices across various social and economic sectors, including education, employment, health, and the justice system. Research indicates that the majority (73%) of Black children and adolescents in public schools fall within high or mid-high poverty levels (Hussar et al., 2020). Findings from the Census Bureau's Household Pulse Survey (HPS) revealed that during the peak of the pandemic in 2020, Latino, Black, and Asian families reported higher rates of financial insecurity and hardship, including job loss, food insecurity, and family instability in housing, compared to White families during the same period (Mitchell, 2020). Additionally, students of color often experience substandard educational conditions and higher rates of disciplinary actions compared to their White peers and those without disabilities, from preschool through high school (U.S. Government Accountability Office [GAO], 2016) (Civil Rights Data Collection, 2021).

The U.S. Department of Education's 2023 Report on the Condition of Education indicated that although American Indian/Alaska Native and African American/Black students comprised a small percentage of total enrollment, they had the highest participation rates in special education under IDEA, with Black students accounting for 17% of those served (Irwin et al., 2023). Black students under IDEA represented 43.5% of all children with disabilities suspended or expelled from school for more than 10 school days, highlighting a persistent and concerning trend. While preschool students of color receiving special education, services constituted only 22.7% of total preschool enrollment, they accounted for 56.9% of preschool children expelled from school (Irwin et al., 2023). This overrepresentation, particularly of Black students, in the special education system, and the evidence suggesting they are excluded from school at higher rates due to their disability than their peers at all education levels, contradicts the 1954 Brown vs. Board of Education of Topeka Supreme Court ruling and subsequent disability rights legislation (Ford et al., 2018).

The intersection of education with health equity and life trajectories is crucial for ensuring the social and economic development of the United States (National Academies of Sciences, Engineering, and Medicine, 2019). Despite decades of federal legislation aiming to provide equal access and participation in schools for disabled children and youth, the impact of the COVID-19 pandemic jeopardizes the futures of students of color served in EI and ECSE programs. Addressing these disparities requires a comprehensive approach to remove institutional and discriminatory barriers in education. First, understanding the legal mandates contributing to these disparities allows for a more nuanced understanding of the systemic issues impacting the education of these already marginalized students in order to develop a more comprehensive service delivery.

Legislation and Disability Rights in Early Childhood Education

The Brown vs. Board of Education of Topeka ruling (1954) was a landmark decision that declared it unlawful to discriminate against individuals based on arbitrary reasons. While this ruling aimed to desegregate schools for Black students, many students with disabilities were still excluded from public schools. Parents of these students used the Brown ruling to advocate for equality, leading to the passage of P.L. 94-142, the Education for All Handicapped Children Act, in 1975 (Ford, 2018). This law, now known as the Individuals with Disabilities Education Act (IDEA), ensured that students with disabilities could receive a free and appropriate public education (FAPE) in the least restrictive environment (LRE).

IDEA Part B (2004) focuses on providing individualized education programs (IEPs) tailored to the unique needs of eligible students with disabilities. These programs outline specific goals, services, and accommodations to help students succeed academically and socially. Part B also mandates schools to provide related services, such as therapy, if necessary for the student's education. The law promotes parent involvement in the IEP development process and provides procedural safeguards to protect their rights.

IDEA Part C (2004) focuses on early intervention services for infants and toddlers with developmental delays or disabilities and their families. This crucial program supports children from birth to age three and aims to identify and address developmental concerns as early as possible. Part C places a strong emphasis on family-centered services, recognizing that parents are essential partners in their child's growth and development. Early intervention services are designed to enhance a child's cognitive, communication, motor, and social-emotional skills during these formative years. These services may include therapies, specialized instruction, and support for parents in understanding and nurturing their child's unique needs. IDEA Part C (2004) aims to give children with developmental delays the best possible start in life, setting them on a trajectory for future success in their educational journey. By intervening early, Part C seeks to minimize potential challenges and maximize each child's potential for positive outcomes.

Part C of the Individuals with Disabilities Education Improvement Act (IDEIA) in 2004 specifically focuses on early intervention services for children facing developmental delays.

Unlike Part B, each state establishes its own criteria for determining eligibility for early intervention, with "developmental delay" being a crucial term individually defined by states for children under three and those aged three to nine. However, the variability in state definitions of 'developmental delay' creates significant challenges, particularly for culturally and linguistically diverse children, who may face additional barriers in accessing timely and appropriate early intervention services. This inconsistency underscores the need for a standardized, equity-focused approach, as advocated in the proposed Bill of Rights.

Developmental delay (DD) is generally characterized as a child not achieving specific milestones in one or more developmental areas (such as communication, motor skills, cognitive abilities, social-emotional skills, or adaptive skills) as expected for typically developing children (Danaher, 2011). It is essential to note that a child's delayed development should not be linked exclusively to a particular condition or diagnosis (e.g., deafness). According to IDEIA (2004), children with DD may qualify for early intervention and related services based on federal and/or state criteria. In Part C of IDEIA (2004), each state defines "developmental delay" for children under the age of three. Additionally, a child with an existing diagnosed physical or mental condition with a high likelihood of DD may also be eligible for early intervention services. Other children demonstrating a delay, as determined by each state, would also meet the criteria for receiving early intervention services.

Presently, states grapple with numerous eligibility issues that impact the number and types of children in need of or receiving services, the nature of services provided, and the costs associated with early intervention services. Consequently, several states have revised their definitions, with some narrowing their eligibility criteria and a few expanding them.

Following the inception of the Early Intervention Program under IDEIA (2004), many states expressed interest in serving children at risk for DD (Danaher, 2011). However, concerns about a significant increase in eligible children and the associated costs led to a reduction in the number of states including at-risk children in their eligibility criteria. Currently, some states not serving at-risk children have expressed the intention to monitor the development of these children and refer them for early intervention services as delays become evident (Danaher, 2011). Overall, IDEA aims to ensure that children with disabilities have equal access to education and the opportunity to reach their full potential. However, its implementation has revealed persistent gaps, particularly in addressing the unique needs of culturally and linguistically diverse students. The inconsistencies in eligibility criteria, coupled with the challenges highlighted by the COVID-19 pandemic, underscore the need for a more comprehensive framework. Therefore, to directly address these gaps and ensure equitable access to culturally responsive services, we propose the following Culturally Responsive Equity-Based Bill of Rights for early intervention and early childhood special education.

Culturally Responsive Equity-Based Bill of Rights for EI and ECSE Children of Color

I. ADVOCACY AND ACCOUNTABILITY

Students of Color with Exceptionalities including early childhood exceptional learners and their families have:

1. The right to inclusive, culturally sustaining and culturally responsive educational policies and procedures grounded in social justice in all academic, behavioral, and social and emotional areas. The right to an administrative structure committed to hiring, supporting, and retaining culturally competent educators of color.
2. The right to be served by culturally competent educators, devoted to ensuring that early childhood students of color with exceptionalities have equitable access to and participation in general, special, and gifted education.
3. The right to be served by culturally competent educators who are committed to drastically reducing the misidentification and misplacement of early childhood students of color with exceptionalities in high incidence categories.

4. The right to be served by educators who are change agents, committed to removing structural and non-structural barriers caused by historical, institutional, and individual biases in service delivery and diagnostic practices.
5. The right to state and district policies that require all college and university preparatory programs to formally prepare/train educators in inclusive pedagogy.
6. Regional, state and district policies that require all college and university preparatory programs to formally train educators in multiculturalism and culturally sustaining, culturally relevant and representative curriculum.
7. The right for those with gifts, talents, special needs, and dual exceptionalities to have access and participate in coordinated family and community collaborations that fully engage with educators in collaborative advocacy processes to promote healthy growth.
8. The right to family and community advocacy groups that act as agents of change to inform state and district leaders. The right to family and community advocacy groups that act as agents of change to inform state and district leaders.
9. The right to an administrative structure that seeks funding for culturally sustaining programming and services in all federally funded programs, including Title I, II, III and IV.
10. The right to guarantee that all equity data are inclusive of opportunities, access, and support within Consolidated States' plans. This includes the Individuals with Disabilities Education Act (IDEA), Every Student Succeeds Act (ESSA) plan (and future legislation), and state-level equity plans.

II. ACCESS TO PROGRAMMING AND SERVICES

Students of Color with Exceptionalities including early childhood exceptional students and their families have:

1. The right to participate in the Least Restrictive Environment (LRE), including early intervention, early childhood special

education, general education programs and services, and gifted education with appropriate accommodations and modifications.
2. The right to equitable access to special education programs, including gifted education, psychological and related services that utilize holistic, asset, and strength-based strategies to facilitate academic, behavioral, social, and emotional learning and well-being.
3. The right to access, and benefit from, district, regional and state level culturally sustaining services that address their strengths and needs.
4. The right to holistic, culturally sustaining services that address the child's exceptionalities, their multiple identities, learning style, cultural strengths, interests, and individual needs.
5. The right to access appropriate enrichment and early intervention educational programs and services—through before-school, after-school, weekend, and summer programs.
6. The right for families to access and participate in culturally sustaining, culturally responsive, enrichment programs in their communities that foster healing and well-being.
7. The right to the development and implementation of culturally sustaining and culturally responsive early childhood education, special education, general education, and gifted program policies and practices that are grounded in social justice, equity based and focused on healing-centered engagement.
8. The right to access, engage in, and benefit from, as needed, free or reduced fee childcare, early intervention, behavioral, psychological, nutritional, and educational programs, and services provided by culturally competent professionals.

III. PROGRAM EVALUATION AND ACCOUNTABILITY

Students of Color with Exceptionalities including early childhood exceptional students have:

1. The right to annual equity goals and objectives for district, regional, and state programs that include strategies for the development, implementation, and evaluation of compensatory services.
2. The right to district, regional, and state program assessments conducted every 3-5 years by external and culturally competent program evaluators with special education expertise.
3. The right to culturally competent teachers who engage in continuous and systematic professional learning experiences focused on holistic, asset- and strength-based culturally sustaining multicultural pedagogy.
4. The right to a culturally sustaining program philosophy/mission/belief statement that explicitly addresses the needs and strengths of early childhood Students of Color at the intersections of race, gender, ethnicity, culture, exceptionality, and socioeconomic status.

IV. EDUCATION, EVALUATION AND ASSESSMENT

Students of Color with Exceptionalities including early childhood exceptional students and their families have:

1. The right to a culturally, racially, and linguistically diverse, equity-based education that promotes safe, culturally sustaining, culturally responsive, holistic, asset- and strength-based evaluation and assessment policies, practices, and protocols.
2. The right to be assessed with tools that reduce and/or eliminate bias inherent in in traditional diagnostic tools, and the use of appropriate practices for students from linguistically and culturally diverse backgrounds who have multiple or traditionally marginalized identities.
3. The right to be assessed for, participate in, and benefit from gifted education even if they have been referred for and/or are served in special education (i.e., thrice

An Equity-Based and Culturally Responsive Bill of Rights

exceptional-students of color who have gifted and special education needs).

4. The right to preparatory programs that train culturally competent early childhood,general, special, pre-service, and current professionals in how to act as change agents dedicated to culturally responsive, inclusive pedagogical practices that recognize and accurately evaluate student differences and expressions of exceptionality.
5. The right to be evaluated and identified for compensatory and special education services using multiple criteria and in multimodal and multi-dimensional ways.
6. The right to be assessed by a culturally competent educator with non-biased tests and instruments; this includes being assessed with a culturally relevant, comprehensive battery of tests for screening and identification.
7. The right to be evaluated by bilingual test examiners (e.g., school psychologists) who act as change agents committed to equity, diversity, inclusion, healing, and well-being.
8. The right to assessments, tests, and instruments in or translated into their predominant or preferred language.
9. The right to be assessed with culturally normed checklists.
10. The right to be evaluated with tools re-normed to represent their cultural experiences, learning styles, and realities.
11. The right to be assessed using tests and instructions that are normed locally.
12. The right to educators committed to social justice and who adhere to culturally responsive current testing and assessment policies and procedures that incorporate student experiences, preferences, interests, needs, and strengths.
13. The right to participate in and benefit from culturally sustaining assessment tools and activities that foster student healing and well-being.

V. EDUCATORS

Students of Color with Exceptionalities including early childhood exceptional students and their families have:

1. The right to early intervention and early childhood educators who act as change agents and are unbiased, culturally competent, committed to culturally responsive teaching practices and healing centered engagement approaches.
2. The right for educators to be properly compensated and receive benefits commensurate with their education, work experience, and job duties.
3. The right to be served by culturally competent early intervention and early childhood educators who have specialized knowledge and skills, and are committed to implementing holistic, asset, strength-based strategies that are culturally sustaining and grounded in social justice.
4. The right to early intervention and early childhood educators committed to creating an inclusive environment that values the education, health, and well-being of all students regardless of learning and behavioral differences.
5. The right for preparatory education programs to train early intervention and early childhood pre-service and current educators to utilize inclusive, culturally sustaining multicultural pedagogy *and* utilize healing centered engagement and instructional strategies that prioritize differential instructional methods.
6. The right to be served by a racially, linguistically, and culturally diverse early intervention, early childhood pre-service and general and special education teaching force composed of professionals who are culturally competent and act as change agents, committed to equity, diversity inclusion, healing, and well-being.
7. The right to have access to and be served by early intervention and early childhood educators of color and community

An Equity-Based and Culturally Responsive Bill of Rights

members who can help advocate for their preferences, interests, needs, and goals.
8. The right to early intervention and early childhood pre-service and current educators who are culturally competent and have bilingual training and credentials.
9. The right to knowledgeable and skilled educators who are culturally competent and have available a range of classroom, after-school, and professional resources (supplies, training options, and health and wellness services, including mental and behavioral health) that meet the diverse needs of students and their families.
10. The right to be served by early childhood professional educators who can utilize instructional approaches and curricula that empower students and families to capitalize on their strengths to facilitate positive development and well-being.

VI. CURRICULUM AND INSTRUCTION

Students of Color with Exceptionalities including early childhood exceptional students and their families have:
1. The right to authentic and multicultural content in all content areas.
2. The right to multicultural curriculum and materials that reflect their cultural, racial, and linguistic background and heritage.
3. The right to culturally sustaining and culturally relevant multicultural curriculum, instruction, activities, materials, and family supports.
4. The right to academic curricula and instructional materials and activities that will help prepare them to reach their fullest potential.
5. The right to authentic multicultural literature reflective of all cultures The right to curricula and materials that promote pride in their abilities, cultural, racial, and linguistic differences.

6. The right to act as their own advocates, that is, for their views to be encouraged and honored rather than silenced and devalued.

VII. SOCIAL AND EMOTIONAL

Students of Color with Exceptionalities including early intervention and early childhood special education students and their families have:
1. The right to supportive and culturally sustaining services and programs by school counselors and educators trained in multicultural counseling (theories, methods, strategies).
2. The right to counselors familiar with and skilled in racial identity theories.
3. The right to counselors who understand and are skilled in disability identity theories and privilege perspectives.
4. The right to counselors and educators who understand the intersectionality of disability (e.g., ability differences) and race.
5. The right to counselors who understand and promote racial and disability identity development.
6. The right to counselors who understand the relationship between achievement and racial and/or disability identity and achievement.
7. The right to counselors and teachers prepared to support the unique challenges of families with children with exceptionalities who are disadvantaged.
8. The right to have formal preparatory programs train pre-service educators, current educators, and counselors on how to meet the socio-emotional needs of children of color with exceptionalities using asset-based approaches.
9. The right to interact and be educated with peers from similar cultural, racial,and linguistic backgrounds.
10. The right to academic and emotional support when they underachieve, fail, and/or make mistakes.

An Equity-Based and Culturally Responsive Bill of Rights

11. The right to have pride in their strengths, cultural heritages, traditions, and beliefs, and accept their individual differences.
12. The right to services and supports that promote participation in self-directed activities to increase opportunities to have their psychological, educational, and transition needs met.

VIII. DISCIPLINE

Students of Color with Exceptionalities including early intervention and early childhood special education students and their families have:

1. The right to discipline grounded in the philosophy and theory of restorative justice.
2. The right to discipline based on culturally responsive principles.
3. The right to dual accountability discipline policies where the goal is to keep students in school, offering them a more nurturing environment that facilitates the development of self-advocacy skills and appropriate problem solving and conflict management.
4. The right to equitable discipline policies and practices that do not feed into the school- to- prison pipeline and that recognize the relationship between behaviors and developmental stages of children and adolescents.
5. The right to access school support services beginning at the first disciplinary interaction.
6. The right to coordinated services and supports that are culturally sustaining, culturally responsive and collaborative among students, families, educators, counselors, and social workers, and aimed at keeping students in school.
7. The right to appropriate behavioral assessments and tiered behavioral supports based on the student's background, needs and interventions.
8. The right to stay in school with adjustments to an existing program or temporary alternative placement that is least

restrictive, educationally and behaviorally beneficial, and in the spirit of advocacy.
9. The right to be educated in a bully-free environment by educators and administrators who are committed to modeling the behaviors, attitudes, and communication they expect from students every day, all day.

IX. FAMILIES AND COMMUNITIES

Students of Color with Exceptionalities including early intervention and early childhood special education students and their families have:
1. The right to educators who value the importance of their families feeling welcome in schools.
2. The right to educators who collaborate with their families and communities.
3. The right to educators who provide professional training to families to strengthen advocacy for their children.
4. The right to have community leaders (e.g., faith leaders, community center leaders) who know and understand them in different contexts involved in the referral, identification, and service delivery process.
5. The right to have their families assist others in the community with understanding the benefits of special education programs and services.
6. The right to have their families serve as 'cultural agents' to inform educators and mediate the cultural mismatch that exists between their communities and dominant culture school personnel.
7. The right for schools to recruit and engage members of their communities who have been successful in serving in the critical roles of mentoring and advocacy.
8. The right for administrative structures that respect the norms, traditions, and culture of communities of color when planning and conducting events.

An Equity-Based and Culturally Responsive Bill of Rights

X. ACCESS TO THE INTERNET AND TECHNOLOGY

Students of Color with Exceptionalities including early intervention and early childhood special education students and their families have:
1. The right to access free internet services and technology tools that support learning and facilitate communication.
2. The right to be taught by culturally competent educators who possess the skills to align technology with a child's developmental level.
3. The right to ongoing professional development for educators, equipping them to use technology effectively, address diverse learning needs, and implement culturally responsive teaching practices.
4. The right to equitable access to high-quality devices and software, ensuring that all students have the same opportunities for educational purposes.
5. The right to personalized learning experiences that consider individual strengths, challenges, and cultural backgrounds.
6. The right to digital educational materials designed to be inclusive and accessible, accommodating students with diverse abilities and learning styles.
7. The right to access assistive technology tools and resources tailored to the specific needs of students with exceptionalities.
8. The right to digital literacy education to allow students and their families to navigate technology responsibly and safely.
9. The right to engage with educators through technology, allowing parents and guardians to stay informed and actively collaborate in their child's education.
10. The right to educational technology that reflects diverse cultural perspectives, languages, and experiences.

References
Brown v. Board of Education, 347 U.S. 483 (1954).
Civil Rights Data Collection, 2021. An Overview of Exclusionary Discipline Practices

in Public Schools for the 2017-2018 School Year. Office for Civil Rights, U.S. Department of Education.

Danaher, J. (2011). Eligibility policies and practices for young children under Part B of IDEA. (NECTAC Notes No. 27). Chapel Hill: The University of North Carolina, FPG Child Development Institute, National Early Childhood Technical Assistance Center.

Ford, D. Y., Dickson, K. T., Davis, J. L., Scott, M. T., & Grantham, T. C. (2018). *A Culturally Responsive Equity-Based Bill of Rights for Gifted Students of Color.* Gifted Child Today, 41(3), 125-129. https://doi.org/10.1177/1076217518769698

Friedman-Krauss, A. H., & Barnett, W. S. (2023). *The state(s) of early intervention and early childhood special education: Looking at equity.* National Institute for Early Education Research. https://nieer.org/policy-landscapes/special-education-report

Hussar, B., Zhang, J., Hein, S., Wang, K., Roberts, A., Cui, J., Smith, M., Bullock Mann, F., Barmer, A., & Dilig, R. (2020). *The condition of education 2020* (NCES 2020-144). National Center for Education Statistics. https://nces.ed.gov/pubsearch/pubsinfo.asp?pubid=2020144

Irwin, V., Wang, K., Tezil, T., Zhang, J., Filbey, A., Jung, J., ... & Parker, S. (2023). *Report on the Condition of Education 2023.* NCES 2023-144. National Center for Education Statistics. https://nces.ed.gov/pubsearch/pubsinfo.asp?pubid=2023144REV

Maier, M., McCormick, M., Morris, P., Nores, M., Phillips, D., & Snow, C. (2021). Historic crisis, historic opportunity: Using evidence to mitigate the effects of the COVID-19 crisis on young children and early care and education programs. University of Michigan and Washington, D.C.: Urban Institute. https://edpolicy.umich.edu/sites/epi/files/2021-07/EPI-UI-Covid Synthesis Brief June 2021.pdfh

Mitchell, F. (2020). *COVID-19's disproportionate effects on children of color will challenge the next generation.* Urban Institute. https://www.urban.org/urban-wire/covid-19s-disproportionate-effects-children-color-will-challenge-next-generation#:~:text=As%20a%20result%2C%20Black%20and,less%20access%20to%20high%2Dquality

National Academies of Sciences, Engineering, and Medicine. (2019). *Vibrant and healthy kids: Aligning science, practice, and policy to advance health equity.* National Academies Press. DOI: https://doi.org/1to0.17226/25466

National Center for Education Statistics. (2021). *The Condition of Education 2021* https://nces.ed.gov/programs/coe/indicator_clb.asp

Sullivan, E. (2021). *The pandemic was disastrous for early childhood education-and both kids and adults are feeling it.* EdSurge. https://www.edsurge.com/news/2021-07-02-the-pandemic-was-disastrous-for-early-childhood-education-and-both-kids-and-adults-are- feeling-it

Individuals With Disabilities Education Act, 20 U.S.C. § 1400 (2004).

Individuals with Disabilities Education Improvement Act, Pub. L. No. 108-446, 118 Stat. 2647 (2004).

United States Government Accountability Office (GAO). (2016, April). *K–12 education: Better use of information could help agencies identify disparities and address racial discrimination (GAO-16-345).* https://www.gao.gov/products/gao-16-345

Book Review: Addressing Anxiety in Young Learners: A Teacher's Guide to Recognizing Needs and Resolving Behaviors

Jacqueline Sperling

Abstract

Since the start of the COVID-19 pandemic, rates of pediatric mental illnesses, especially anxiety disorders, have increased significantly (Racine et al., 2021), and with this change, teachers have been tasked with educating even more students who have additional needs. *Addressing Anxiety in Young Learners: A Teacher's Guide to Recognizing Needs and Resolving Behaviors* is a book that aims to provide teachers with an understanding of pediatric anxiety disorders and practical tools to support students who present with symptoms of them. The following review of the book describes what the book addresses, highlights strengths, examines areas for improvement, and offers additional and different perspectives on pediatric anxiety disorders.

Keywords: Anxiety disorders, children, teachers, education, and assessment

Overview

The 135-page book, which includes the index, costs $29.95 in the United States at the time of production and is intended for teachers of students ages three to eight. It was written by Sarah Taylor Vanover, Ed.D. and Kristen Mennona, L.P.C., B.C.-D.M.T., C.E.D.S. and published by Paul H. Brookes Publishing Co. in 2024. The book begins with a case example of a child with mental illness and additional needs in the classroom. Next, the book orients readers to developmental milestones to help set expectations for an average course of growth. Afterward, the book provides information on generalized anxiety disorder (GAD), separation anxiety disorder, social anxiety disorder, selective mutism, obsessive-compulsive disorder (OCD), specific phobias, post-traumatic stress disorder (PTSD), depressive disorders, autism spectrum disorder, attention-deficit/hyperactivity disorder (AD/HD), and mood disorders. In each section, diagnostic criteria are reviewed, relevant treatments for outside of school are discussed, the role of teachers is explained, and a case example that describes the presentation of symptoms and supports involved are discussed. Next, there is a review of how to partner with parents, which strategies to implement in the classroom, and which approaches to avoid using. The book concludes with one final case example that incorporates all the information mentioned in the book followed by references and an index.

Authors importantly offered guidelines for understanding cognitive, speech and language, motor and physical, and social and emotional developmental trajectories so teachers can assess whether or not students are on track, and the book reviewed the milestones for different ages. This book review will highlight areas that need further clarification. For example, when discussing developmental milestones, the text noted that if a child skips crawling, then the child will have gait issues in the future. However, this is not always the case, and the absence of crawling should be investigated if other delays or motor abnormalities are present (Movement: Babies 8 to 12 months, 2021).

As another example of clarification that this review will offer, the critical learning period for learning new languages described was briefer than is suggested by research. Authors indicated that the period ends at age 3.5, but research has found that it goes up to 17.4 years of age (Hartshorne et al., 2018).

Diagnoses and Treatments

Generalized anxiety disorder (GAD), which involves difficult-to-control worries in multiple domains for most days of the week for at least six months, can occur with physiological symptoms, such as restlessness, tension, or fatigue, irritability, and disruptions to sleep and concentration (American Psychiatric Association, 2013). GAD, the first anxiety disorder discussed in the book, was described as the most common anxiety disorder, but specific phobias are the most prevalent (Kowalchuk et al., 2022). In addition, the diagnostic criteria for GAD included the need for the symptoms to affect two or more relationships, but that is not needed per se. Instead, the criteria include a need for interference in areas of functioning. Furthermore, the symptom duration was inaccurately listed as two months when it is six months (American Psychiatric Association, 2013). Moreover, comorbid diagnoses were described incorrectly. Attention-Deficit disorder was listed in addition to AD/HD, but the former is not a disorder. Instead, there are subtypes of AD/HD. Disruptive behavior disorder also was listed; disruptive disorders is a category of disorders rather than a diagnosis (American Psychiatric Association, 2013).

In the discussion of evidence-based treatments for GAD, authors listed play therapy; however cognitive behavioral therapy (CBT) is the *well-established* treatment. Although CBT was mentioned for separation anxiety disorder, it was described as a form of "talk therapy," and authors did not describe CBT's behavioral nature or the specific type of CBT used for separation anxiety disorder and other anxiety disorders, exposure therapy or exposure and response prevention (ERP) treatment, which are evidence-based (Higa-McMillan et al., 2016).

After GAD, authors discussed separation anxiety disorder, which involves a fear lasting at least four weeks about something harmful happening to the child or loved ones upon separation. Children may refuse to separate from caregivers within or outside of the house, and they may experience somatic symptoms, such as stomachaches, when anticipating separation, as well as frequent nightmares related to the fear (American Psychiatric Association, 2013). The book included inaccuracies regarding the diagnostic criteria for separation anxiety disorder. Specifically, the fear was described as being worried about separating from home or a loved one. It is key to specify that the fear is about harm happening to the child or loved ones upon separation. Children may worry about separating from parents when they have symptoms of other disorders, such as when parents are safety behaviors, people or objects thought to help prevent feared outcomes but interfere with one learning that they can handle experiences without them, for children who have agoraphobia. Furthermore, bedwetting and irritability were mistakenly listed as diagnostic criteria (American Psychiatric Association, 2013). Authors also noted that separation anxiety disorder can predict the onset of GAD, but the most common subsequent concerns are panic and depressive disorders (Lewinsohn et al., 2008).

Next, social anxiety disorder, a concern about being judged or embarrassed, especially by peers, to the point that it interferes with experiences for at least six months (American Psychiatric Association, 2013), was reviewed. Inaccuracies were present in the social anxiety disorder section, as well. For instance, authors declared that situations listed always occur when those just are some examples of how social anxiety disorder manifests. It also was noted that the symptoms must be present in multiple situations, but one can have a performance subtype of social anxiety disorder. In addition, the duration of symptoms in the diagnostic criteria was listed as two months when the symptoms need to have persisted for six months to meet full criteria for the disorder. It also is important to clarify that the fear of judgment or embarrassment at least must concern social situations with peers (American Psychiatric Association, 2013). Furthermore, physiological symptoms were listed as part of the diagnostic criteria. They are not required, but those with social anxiety disorder can have cued panic attacks as a qualifier for the diagnosis (American Psychiatric Association, 2013).

Authors mentioned that those with shy temperaments are more likely to develop social anxiety disorder. The temperament that has been associated with the subsequent development of the disorder is behavioral inhibition, and it includes a reticence to try new experiences in general and not just social ones (Clauss & Blackford, 2012).

When treatment for social anxiety disorder was discussed, authors noted that providers will wait until the symptoms have been present for at least two months. However, if the symptoms interfere with a child's functioning, a provider can diagnose and treat someone with other specified anxiety disorder and note that the symptoms have not been present for six months to meet criteria for social anxiety disorder (American Psychiatric Association, 2013).

The book next reviewed selective mutism, which involves a child, who has the capacity to speak, not speaking in most social situations for at least a month (American Psychiatric Association, 2013). The one-month duration of selective mutism symptoms criterion was absent in the book (American Psychiatric Association, 2013). In addition, authors noted that the disorder can persist if left untreated, which is accurate (Keeton, 2013). However, subsequently, authors contradicted that statement by noting that the duration of selective mutism is eight years.

Authors importantly encouraged adults to respond consistently to children with selective mutism; however, authors recommended that adults reinforce non-verbal behaviors. Instead, it is key for adults to provide forced-choice questions so that children are encouraged to speak responses (Furr et al., 2020).

Authors described CBT as a treatment that is more appropriate for older children, but CBT can be used with young children (Oerbeck et al., 2015). In addition, play therapy was mentioned as a treatment for selective mutism, but it is not one of the gold standards of treatment for selective mutism. CBT, individual or group-based behavioral treatment, and parent-child interaction therapy for selective mutism are evidence-based treatments (Lorenzo et al., 2020).

In the section that described anxiety disorders, panic disorder and agoraphobia were missing. However, OCD and PTSD were included. Although OCD and PTSD were formerly categorized as anxiety disorders, the diagnoses in 2013 were moved into two different categories, obsessive-compulsive and related disorders and trauma and stressor-related disorders respectively (American Psychiatric Association, 2013).

OCD is a disorder that involves intrusive obsessions that cause distress, and children may attempt to reduce the distress by engaging in mental or observable rituals that either take up at least an hour a day or at least cause significant interference (American Psychiatric Association, 2013). In the book's description of OCD, authors asserted that children fear something bad will happen if they do not do a certain ritual. It is important to mention that children sometimes have rituals that are based on feeling "just right" instead of preventing a feared outcome (Scahill et al., 1997). In addition, the duration of symptoms was not specified, which as mentioned above, must either take up one hour a day or at least cause significant distress or interference (American Psychiatric Association, 2013). With respect to causes, it is worth stating that OCD also can be precipitated by infections (Cocuzza et al., 2022) so that teachers can be aware of cases that involve sudden onsets of symptoms.

Authors next transitioned to discussing specific phobias, which are fears of discrete objects or situations that interfere with functioning for at least six months (American Psychiatric Association, 2013), and stated that panic attacks are part of the diagnostic criteria. The panic attacks are not required, though children can experience cued panic attack symptoms when faced with their feared stimuli (American Psychiatric Association, 2013). Authors noted that anxiety is a heritable trait when causes were discussed. It is important to clarify that all humans experience fear and anxiety (Steimer et al., 2002), but children may be born with a genetic predisposition to developing an anxiety disorder (Strawn et al., 2021).

Play therapy was mentioned again as an evidence-based treatment for specific phobias, and treatment also was described as more of a long-term process that needs to be attended consistently in order for gains to be made. Although the description of the latter is important for treatment in general, evidence-based treatment for specific phobias has been found to be effective in a single extended session of CBT with ERP (Davis et al., 2019). In addition, authors encouraged parents to provide reassurance as part of the treatment, and that is contraindicated because reassurance can negatively reinforce anxiety (Chiappini et al., 2021).

After specific phobias, the book focused on trauma and PTSD. The book asserted that there is no specific way to define trauma and that divorce is an example of a traumatic event. Traumatic events, however, are defined in the diagnostic criteria for posttraumatic stress disorder and include experiences that threaten a child's safety or ones in which a child witnesses loved ones' safety at risk (American Psychiatric Association, 2013). Divorce can be an adverse experience but is not necessarily always traumatic. Regarding PTSD, children may meet criteria if they have been exposed to a traumatic event, have intrusive reexperiencing symptoms, such as flashbacks or nightmares, avoid reminders of the traumatic event(s), and have at least two different changes in their physiological responses, such as hypervigilance and an exaggerated startle response for at least one month. For children older than six years of age, there also would be a presence of at least two negative changes in cognition and mood, such as persistent negative believes about themselves, others, and the world and certain emotional states, such as shame (American Psychiatric Association, 2013). The diagnostic criteria in the book included inaccuracies; some experiences listed are not required, such as difficulty making friends, while others were absent, including the categories of symptoms mentioned previously (American Psychiatric Association, 2013).

With respect to treatment for PTSD, EMDR was noted as evidence-based, and it is important to mention that trauma-focused CBT has more evidence than EMDR for effectiveness in the pediatric population (Mavranezouli et al, 2020). Furthermore, the book mentioned that psychologists only do assessments for children when there may be concerns about how mental illness may be impacting school performance. That often is psychologists' role in schools, but it is important to clarify that clinical psychologists also are trained to provide treatment.

Comorbid Diagnoses and Treatments

Comorbid diagnoses are those that co-occur, and it is very common for youth to experience more than one mental illness at a time. For example, research on adolescents found that 40% experienced comorbid diagnoses (Merikangas et al., 2010). Authors mentioned depression is a common comorbid concern for children with anxiety disorders. It would have been helpful to describe the specific types of depressive disorders, such as major depressive disorder and persistent depressive disorder. In addition, how depression may manifest as irritability in children was missing. Some diagnostic criteria also were omitted, such as psychomotor retardation, and other symptoms that are not part of the criteria were included instead, such as stomachaches (American Psychiatric Association, 2013).

For the discussion of autism spectrum disorder as another common comorbid diagnosis, authors excluded the restricted interest and repetitive behaviors category of symptoms. Authors also used the term dual-diagnosis to describe one having multiple mental health illnesses. Typically, that term is reserved for those experiencing a substance use disorder in addition to another mental illness (Cleveland Clinic, 2024).

Collaboration With Parents

Authors importantly highlighted how parents may need to grieve after learning that their child has a mental illness, and the book described a linear bereavement process. In order to normalize variability in the grieving process, it is critical to mention that the process is not linear. Parents can go through the stages of grief in different orders and not necessarily experience all of the stages (The Five Stages of Grief, 2024). In addition to processing loss, authors supported parental advocacy for children and highlighted the different emotionally salient efforts that parents often have to put forth when seeking support for their children, such as advocating for insurance coverage of therapeutic services. It seems that there may have been a minor typographical error in the advocacy section that meant to say that it is *not* always possible to change insurance companies' decisions.

Strengths

A notable strength of this book is that it guides teachers on what their roles are when a student with a mental illness needs an assessment at school and/or receives treatment outside of school. For example, authors recommended that teachers act as observers and share data without diagnosing a child or making treatment recommendations. There was a key emphasis on partnering with parents and supporting the treatment paths that parents pursue so that teachers can act as collaborators. The book importantly suggested that teachers share students' strengths in addition to challenges at meetings with parents when a teacher has concerns about how a child's mental health may be impacting the child's school experience. Authors also astutely encouraged teachers to avoid supporting avoidance and instead, facilitate new experiences in order not to strengthen anxiety disorders.

Another strength is the book's guidance for teachers on how to start the year by setting rules and then following through with logical consequences to manage noncompliance. Authors also wisely suggested that teachers help children practice new tools while feeling calm so that they can use them when in more emotionally salient situations. Authors shared several specific mindfulness and relaxation skills that teachers can share with children. It is important to note when to use each of the skills. Mindfulness is indicated during a panic attack or other exposures to anxiety so that children can learn that there is not a threat to their safety and that they can handle the situation. Relaxation skills can be used during lower levels of anxiety and well before stressful situations, but not during a panic attack or exposures because they disrupt the learning process that there is the absence of an intolerable safety threat (Craske et al., 2014).

Furthermore, authors shared recommendations for how to manage children with social anxiety disorder in the classroom. Some of the accommodations mentioned actually negatively reinforce avoidance, so it is important to note that if these accommodations were to be implemented, they should be temporary and used while the child gradually works on increasing levels of engagement as part of treatment. For example, a teacher temporarily may refrain from calling on a student without a raised hand until that student works up to participating more in class. Moreover, the book critically emphasized that even if a student's mental illness may not interfere during the school day, that does not mean that the school is adequately meeting the child's needs, such as a child who reserves expressing their distress or struggles to complete homework outside of school.

Growth Areas

An area of growth for the book is to incorporate how to create culturally responsive approaches to supporting children in the classroom as well as identity considerations. For example, authors alternated between binary gender pronouns and did not acknowledge that there may be other pronouns used. It also is important to consider that some children may have caregivers who are not parents, and to acknowledge that there may be different perspectives about mental health depending on how caregivers identify.

It also is key to model the behavior descriptions the book encourages teachers to do by refraining from using judgmental language, such as "meltdowns." The book did use strength- based language regarding development trajectories, such as strengths and areas for growth; however, several pages later, the growth areas were labeled as "weaknesses" instead, and mental health diagnoses were declared as permanent. It actually is possible for mental health diagnoses to go into remission. For example, researchers have found that 59% percent of youth with anxiety disorders who received CBT experienced remission after treatment (Levy et al., 2022).

Despite some areas for improvement, the book highlights the need to support children with anxiety disorders effectively in classrooms and offers concrete strategies for teachers in the twelfth chapter. With adjustments to enhance the accuracy of the information presented, the book could provide teachers with valuable resources to help children make the most of their experiences at school.

References

American Psychiatric Association. (2013). *Diagnostic and statistical manual of mental disorders* (5th ed.). https://doi.org/10.1176/appi.books.9780890425596.

Chiappini, E. A., Parrish, C., Reynolds, E., & McGuire, J. F. (2021). Overcoming barriers in cognitive-behavioral therapy for youth anxiety and obsessive- compulsive disorder: Addressing parent behaviors. *Bulletin of the Menninger Clinic, 85*(3), 231–253. https://doi.org/10.1521/bumc.2021.85.3.231.

Clauss, J. A., & Blackford, J. U. (2012). Behavioral inhibition and risk for developing social anxiety disorder: a meta-analytic study. *Journal of the American Academy of Child and Adolescent Psychiatry, 51*(10), 1066–1075.e1. https://doi.org/10.1016/j.jaac.2012.08.002.

Cleveland Clinic. *Dual diagnosis*. Retrieved January 17, 2024, from https://my.clevelandclinic.org/health/diseases/24426-dual-diagnosis.

Cocuzza, S., Maniaci, A., La Mantia, I., Nocera, F., Caruso, D., Caruso, S., Iannella, G., Vicini, C., Privitera, E., Lechien, J. R., & Pavone, P. (2022). Obsessive- compulsive disorder in PANS/PANDAS in children: In search of a qualified treatment-a systematic review and metanalysis. *Children (Basel,Switzerland), 9(2)*, 155. https://doi.org/10.3390/children9020155.

Craske, M. G., Treanor, M., Conway, C. C., Zbozinek, T., & Vervliet, B. (2014). Maximizing exposure therapy: An inhibitory learning approach. *Behaviour research and therapy, 58*, 10–23. https://doi.org/10.1016/j.brat.2014.04.006.

Davis, T. E., 3rd, Ollendick, T. H., & Öst, L. G. (2019). One-session treatment of specific phobias in children: Recent developments and a systematic review. *Annual Review of Clinical Psychology, 15*, 233–256. https://doi.org/10.1146/annurev-clinpsy-050718-095608.

Furr, J. M., Sanchez, A. L., Hong, N., & Comer, J. S. (2020). Exposure therapy for childhood selective mutism: Principles, practices, and procedures. In T. S. Peris, E. A. Storch, & J. F. McGuire (Eds.), *Exposure therapy for children with anxiety and OCD: Clinician's guide to integrated treatment* (pp. 113–142). Elsevier Academic Press. https://doi.org/10.1016/B978-0-12-815915-6.00006-8.

Hartshorne, J. K., Tenenbaum, J. B., & Pinker, S. (2018). A critical period for second language acquisition: Evidence from 2/3 million English speakers. *Cognition, 177,* 263–277. https://doi.org/10.1016/j.cognition.2018.04.007.

Higa-McMillan, C. K., Francis, S. E., Rith-Najarian, L., & Chorpita, B. F. (2016). Evidence Base Update: 50 years of research on treatment for child and adolescent anxiety. *Journal of Clinical Child and Adolescent Psychology, 45*(2), 91–113. https://doi.org/10.1080/15374416.2015.1046177)

Keeton, C.P. (2013). Selective mutism. In: Vasa, R. Roy, A. (Eds.), *Pediatric anxiety disorders: A clinical guide.* (pp. 209-227). Humana Press. https://doi.org/10.1007/978-1-4614-6599-7_11.

Kowalchuk, A. Gonzalez, S.J., & Zoorob, R.J. (2022). Anxiety disorders in children and adolescents. *American Family Physician, 106*(6), 657-664.

Levy, H. C., Stevens, K. T., & Tolin, D. F. (2022). Research Review: A meta-analysis of relapse rates in cognitive behavioral therapy for anxiety and related disorders in youth. *Journal of Child Psychology and Psychiatry, and Allied Disciplines, 63*(3), 252–260. https://doi.org/10.1111/jcpp.13486.

Lewinsohn, P. M., Holm-Denoma, J. M., Small, J. W., Seeley, J. R., & Joiner, T. E., Jr. (2008). Separation anxiety disorder in childhood as a risk factor for future mental illness. *Journal of the American Academy of Child and Adolescent Psychiatry, 47*(5), 548–555. https://doi.org/10.1097/CHI.0b013e31816765e7.

Lorenzo, N.E., Cornacchio, D., Chou, T., Kurtz, S.M., Furr, J.M., & Comer, J.S. (2020). Expanding treatment options for children with selective mutism: Rationale, principles, and procedures for an intensive group behavioral treatment. *Cognitive and Behavioral Practice.* https://doi.org/10.1016/j.cbpra.2020.06.002.

Mavranezouli, I., Megnin-Viggars, O., Daly, C., Dias, S., Stockton, S., Meiser- Stedman, R., Trickey, D., & Pilling, S. (2020). Research review: Psychological and psychosocial treatments for children and young people with post-traumatic stress disorder: a network meta-analysis. *Journal of Child Psychology and Psychiatry, and Allied Disciplines, 61*(1), 18–29. https://doi.org/10.1111/jcpp.13094.

Merikangas, K. R., He, J. P., Burstein, M., Swanson, S. A., Avenevoli, S., Cui, L., Benjet, C., Georgiades, K., & Swendsen, J. (2010). Lifetime prevalence of mental disorders in U.S. adolescents: Results from the National Comorbidity Survey Replication--Adolescent Supplement (NCS-A). *Journal of the American Academy of Child and Adolescent Psychiatry, 49*(10), 980–989. https://doi.org/10.1016/j.jaac.2010.05.017.

Movement: Babies 8 to 12 months. (2021, April 7). Healthy Children. Retrieved January 11, 2024, from https://www.healthychildren.org/English/ages-stages/baby/Pages/Movement-8-to-12-Months.aspx?_gl=1*ysir3m*_ga*MTUxNjMyMzIwMi4xNzA0OTk2OTgy*_ga_FD9D3XZVQQ*MTcwNTUxNjI0NS4zLjAuMTcwNTUxNjI0NS4wLjAuMA.

Oerbeck, B., Stein, M.B., Pripp, A.H., & Kristensen, H. (2015). Selective mutism: Follow-up study 1 year after end of treatment. *European Child & Adolescent Psychiatry, 24*, 757–766. https://doi.org/10.1007/s00787-014-0620-1.

Racine, N., McArthur, B.A., Cooke, J.E., Eirich, R., Zhu, J., & Madigan, S. (2021). Global prevalence of depressive and anxiety symptoms in children and adolescents during COVID- 19: A meta-analysis. *JAMA Pediatrics, 175(11),* 1142-1150. https://doi.org/10.1001/jamapediatrics.2021.2482.

Scahill, L., Riddle, M.A., McSwiggin-Hardin, M., Ort, S.I., King, R.A., Goodman, W.K., Cicchetti, D. & Leckman, J.F. (1997). Children's Yale-Brown Obsessive Compulsive Scale: Reliability and validity. *Journal of the American Academy of Child and Adolescent Psychiatry, 36*(6), 844–852. https://doi.org/10.1097/00004583-199706000-00023.

Steimer T. (2002). The biology of fear- and anxiety-related behaviors. *Dialogues in Clinical Neuroscience, 4*(3), 231–249. https://doi.org/10.31887/DCNS.2002.4.3/tsteimer. The five stages of grief. Grief. Retrieved January 17, 2024, from https://grief.com/the-five-stages-of-grief/.

Strawn, J. R., Lu, L., Peris, T. S., Levine, A., & Walkup, J. T. (2021). Research Review: Pediatric anxiety disorders - what have we learnt in the last 10 years? *Journal of Child Psychology and Psychiatry, and Allied Disciplines, 62*(2), 114–139. https://doi.org/10.1111/jcpp.13262.

List of Contibutors

Mildred Boveda, Ed.D., is an Associate Professor of the Special Education program at Penn State University. Her research focuses on preparing educators to work effectively with students from diverse backgrounds by developing the concepts of "intersectional competence" and "intersectional consciousness." These frameworks help assess how teachers understand and respond to the multiple, intersecting sociocultural identities of students, families, and colleagues. She is the creator of the Intersectional Competence Measure and grounds her work in Black feminist epistemology, exploring how theoretical and empirical approaches can inform justice-oriented educational practice.

Dr. Boveda holds an Ed.D. in Exceptional Student Education from Florida International University and an Ed.M. in Education Policy and Management from Harvard University. She serves as co-editor of the *Review of Educational Research*, a flagship journal of the American Educational Research Association (AERA), and has held leadership positions including Program Co-Chair of AERA Division K and past president of the Council for Exceptional Children's Division for Diverse and Exceptional Learners. Her scholarship, teaching, and advocacy emphasize equity, teacher learning, and the transformative possibilities of intersectional frameworks.

Qunishia N. Carter, Ph.D., is an educational psychologist who earned her Ph.D. in Educational Psychology from Ball State University. Her research examines the experiences of Black women in higher education, with a focus on socialization, identity development, and the role of counter-spaces in fostering resilience and academic persistence. She is particularly interested in how systemic and contextual factors—such as race, bias, and belonging—shape educational outcomes across the lifespan. In addition to her work in higher education, Dr. Carter contributes to research addressing early educational disparities and disciplinary inequities affecting young children from marginalized communities. She is currently pursuing postdoctoral opportunities that allow her to further examine equity-driven approaches across educational systems.

Kathryn L. Fletcher, Ph.D., is a professor of psychology in the Department of Educational Psychology at Ball State University, Muncie, Indiana. She received her Ph.D. in Developmental Psychology from the University of Alabama at Birmingham. Dr. Fletcher has expertise in child development and educational psychology, with peer-reviewed articles in the areas of early literacy and language development, perfectionism, and the impact of parenting and perfectionism on academic motivation. Dr. Fletcher serves on the editorial board of several scholarly journals and is active in schools and community organizations to support children's school readiness and academic success.

Donna Y. Ford, Ph.D., is a Distinguished Professor of Education and Human Ecology in the College of Education and Human Ecology at the Ohio State University. She is also a Faculty Affiliate with the Kirwan Institute and the Center for Latin American Studies. Professor Ford is in the Department of Educational Studies and the Special Education Program.

Professor Ford conducts research primarily in gifted education and culturally responsive/multicultural/urban education. Specifically, her work focuses on: (1) the achievement gap; (2) recruiting and retaining culturally different students in gifted education; (3) multicultural curriculum and instruction; (4) culturally competent teacher training and development; (5) African-American identity; and (6) African-American family involvement. She consults with school districts, and educational and legal organizations on such topics as gifted education under-representation and Advanced Placement, multicultural/urban education and counseling, and closing the achievement gap.

Colleen D. Martinez, Ph.D., is an Assistant Professor of Social Work at Ramapo College of New Jersey where she teaches theory, life cycle development, research, and play therapy courses. She is also a practicing Licensed Clinical Social Worker and Registered

Play Therapist Supervisor. Dr. Martinez is particularly interested in early childhood mental health and what families, systems, and structures can do to promote early childhood mental health and wellness. Through her teaching, scholarship, supervision, and consultation she aims to help more children and families receive high quality developmentally appropriate supports and services.
Email: cmarti13@ramapo.edu

Michelle Frazier Trotman Scott, Ph.D., is the Director of Doctoral Programs and Professor of Special Education at the University of West Georgia. Dr. FTS writes, presents, and facilitates workshops and dialogues on various topics, including educational practices and reform, effective and transformative leadership, leadership development and mentoring, time management, productivity, and topics related to inclusivity, acceptance, and belonging. She has also written extensively about disproportionalities in gifted and special education, dual exceptionalities, the achievement gap, cultural responsiveness, and familial involvement. She has served and led in multiple professional organizations and currently serves on the NAGC Board of Directors as the Governance Secretary. She is the winner of the R.A.C.E. Mentoring Founders Award and the Inaugural Council for Exceptional Children–TAG Diversity Award.

Evette Simmons-Reed, Ph.D., is the Program Director for the Disability in Postsecondary Settings Graduate Certificate Program with an emphasis in Autism, and the Director and Co-Founder of the CAPS2 Mentor Program for Autistic College Students at the Ball State Center for Autism Spectrum Disorder (CASD) at Ball State University. Prior to joining the faculty at BSU, she was the Program Manager in the Special Education and Transition Department at The Ohio State University in Columbus, Ohio, where she oversaw the development and implementation of a 2.5 million dollar federally funded demonstration project for students with intellectual and developmental disabilities. As a social justice advocate, her professional interests involve incorporation of culturally sustaining practices in special education, disproportionality, universal design for learning, and transition. Her research and expertise focus on leveraging resources to support equitable access and participation of autistic and intellectually disabled young adults in higher education in order to improve their quality-of-life outcomes. Currently, she is the principal investigator for a National Institute of Health (NIH) grant to help customize a conversational agent or avatar, that will serve as a remote digital companion and coach for autistic young adults.

Jacqueline Sperling, Ph.D., is a clinical psychologist, faculty at Harvard Medical School, and the co-founder and Co-Program Director of the McLean Anxiety Mastery Program at McLean Hospital. She also is the author of the young adult nonfiction book *Find Your Fierce: How to Put Social Anxiety in Its Place* and a contributor for Harvard Health Publishing. Dr. Sperling specializes in implementing evidence-based treatments, such as cognitive behavioral therapy, and working with youth who present with anxiety disorders and/or obsessive-compulsive disorder. She also focuses on providing parent guidance by using treatments, such as behavioral parent training.

Gloria Taradash holds a Ph.D. in special education with an emphasis on gifted minorities and families. She served on the board of directors of the National Association for Gifted Children (NAGC) and as president of the Special Populations Network. In the Council for Exceptional Children (CEC) she served as president of The Association for the Gifted (TAG), where she received the Outstanding Service Award and as president of the Culturally and Linguistically Diverse Exceptional Learners Network (DDEL), where she was awarded the Dr. Alexinia Baldwin Gifted & ___ Award. She served on the board of directors of the Black Caucus of Special Educators. She has presented at local, state, national, and international conferences on issues of gifted diversity and families.

Dr. Taradash has served as a reviewer for the Journal for the Education of the Gifted, Gifted Child Quarterly, and the Journal of Secondary Gifted Education. During her tenure as president of the New Mexico Association for the Gifted and the Albuquerque

Association for Gifted and Talented Students, she organized parent groups for gifted children across the state of New Mexico.

Beth Trammell, Ph.D., is a Professor of Psychology at Indiana University East where she is the Director of the Master of Arts in Mental Health Counseling program. She is a licensed psychologist with 20 years of experience working with kids and families. She currently specializes in behavioral and communication strategies for parents and teachers, with special emphasis in early childhood. She believes focusing on very young children is the key to decreasing later mental health issues, which is why she has been using podcasts, workshops, and webinars to help the adults who are around kids to be better equipped for this next generation. She has specific research interests in antecedent strategies to behavior management, restorative practices, and mental wellness.

Perspectives on Early Childhood Psychology and Education

PECPE publishes twice a year, in the fall and spring. These two issues on specific focuses are typically guest-edited and can also include a few general articles.

Editorial Policy and Submission Guidelines

Perspectives on Early Childhood Psychology and Education focuses on publishing original contributions from a broad range of psychological and educational perspectives relevant to infants, young children (to age 8 years), families, and caregivers. Manuscripts incorporating evidence-based research, theory, and practice within clinical, community, developmental, neurological, and school psychology perspectives are considered. In addition, the journal accepts test and book reviews, literature reviews, program descriptions and evaluations, clinical studies, and other professional materials of interest to psychologists and educators working with young children. Proposals for special focus topics may be made to the Editor.

Format: Manuscripts should be original work not currently submitted for publication to other journals. Authors must follow the guidelines of the Publication Manual of the American Psychological Association (Sixth Edition). Manuscripts may not exceed 35 double-spaced pages in length, including the cover page, abstract, references, tables, and figures.

Submission: Submit an electronic copy of the manuscript for editorial review. Avoid including any identifying author information in the text. Selection of manuscripts is based on blind peer review. Include a cover page with the following information: the title of article, author(s) full name(s), title(s), institution or professional affiliations, and mailing and email address of primary author. The cover page will not be sent to reviewers.

Selection Criteria:
- Importance of topic in early childhood psychology and education
- Theory and research related to content
- Contribution to professional practice in early childhood psychology and education
- Clear and concise writing
- Submit manuscripts to the Editor electronically at the following email address: PECPE@bsu.edu.

Call for Submissions!

The journal Perspectives on Early Childhood Psychology and Education (PECPE) is now accepting submissions for a special issue titled "Whole Child Ready: Advancing Critical Perspectives in Early Childhood Education."

Papers may include original research, literature reviews, policy analyses, and theoretical pieces that offer innovative perspectives on the intersection of family, community, culture, and policy in early childhood education.

For questions or more information please contact the co-guest editors for this special issue, Dr. Jill Walls (jkwalls2@bsu.edu) and Dr. Jiyeon Lee (jiyeon.lee@bsu.edu).

Submission Topics Include:
- Early Childhood Education
- The Meaning of Kindergarten Readiness
- The Broader Systems that Influence Children's Success in School

Submit your paper here!

Volume 9, Issue 1 of
Perspectives on Early Childhood Psychology and Education
was published in Spring 2025
by Pace University Press

Cover and interior layout by Zetta Whiting
The journal was typeset in Minion and Myriad
and printed by Lightning Source

Pace University Press

Director: Manuela Soares
Faculty Advisor: Eileen Kreit
Design Consultant: Joseph Caserto

Graduate Assistants: Vidhi Sampat and Zetta Whiting
Graduate Student Aide: Kianna Swingle